T0340600

OPEN TO
REASON

RELIGION, CULTURE, AND PUBLIC LIFE

RELIGION, CULTURE, AND PUBLIC LIFE

SERIES EDITOR: KATHERINE PRATT EWING

The resurgence of religion calls for careful analysis and constructive criticism of new forms of intolerance, as well as new approaches to tolerance, respect, mutual understanding, and accommodation. In order to promote serious scholarship and informed debate, the Institute for Religion, Culture, and Public Life and Columbia University Press are sponsoring a book series devoted to the investigation of the role of religion in society and culture today. This series includes works by scholars in religious studies, political science, history, cultural anthropology, economics, social psychology, and other allied fields whose work sustains multidisciplinary and comparative as well as transnational analyses of historical and contemporary issues. The series focuses on issues related to questions of difference, identity, and practice within local, national, and international contexts. Special attention is paid to the ways in which religious traditions encourage conflict, violence, and intolerance and also support human rights, ecumenical values, and mutual understanding. By mediating alternative methodologies and different religious, social, and cultural traditions, books published in this series will open channels of communication that facilitate critical analysis.

For a complete list see page 121.

OPEN TO REASON

MUSLIM PHILOSOPHERS IN CONVERSATION WITH THE WESTERN TRADITION

SOULEYMANE BACHIR DIAGNE

Translated by
JONATHAN ADJEMIAN

Columbia University Press
New York

Columbia University Press
Publishers Since 1893
New York   Chichester, West Sussex
cup.columbia.edu

Library of Congress Cataloging-in-Publication Data
Names: Diagne, Souleymane Bachir, author. | Adjemian,
    Jonathan, translator.
Title: Open to reason: Muslim philosophers in conversation
    with the Western tradition / Souleymane Bachir Diagne;
    translated by Jonathan Adjemian.
Other titles: Comment philosopher en islam. English
Description: New York: Columbia University Press, [2018] | Series:
    Religion, culture, and public life | Translation of: Comment
    philosopher en islam. | Includes bibliographical references
    and index.
Identifiers: LCCN 2018009493 | ISBN 9780231185462 (cloth: alk. paper) |
    ISBN 9780231546171 (e-book)
Subjects: LCSH: Islam and philosophy. | Islamic philosophy. |
    Philosophy and religion.
Classification: LCC BP163 .D5213 2018 | DDC 181/.07—dc23
LC record available at https://lccn.loc.gov/2018009493

Cover design: Milenda Nan Ok Lee
Cover art: Kader Attia, *Black Cube*, 2005. Oil on canvas, 200 x 200 cm.
Photo Kader Attia. Courtesy of the artist and Galerie Nagel Draxler.

CONTENTS

Acknowledgments   vii
Introduction   ix

1. And How to Not Philosophize?   1

2. How a Language Becomes Philosophical   14

3. What Does It Mean for a Philosophy to Be Islamic?   23

4. Against Philosophy?   35

5. A Lesson in Ecological Philosophy   46

6. The Obligation to Philosophize   55

7. The Need for Philosophy   67

8. The Philosophy of Reform   76

9. The Philosophy of Movement   85

10. Pluralism   98

Conclusion   102

Notes   105
Bibliography   113
Index   117

ACKNOWLEDGMENTS

I have to thank many people for this book. Roger-Pol Droit was the first to publish the French original. Felwine Sarr and Philippe Rey then published a new edition. Jonathan Adjemian has made the English translation thanks to the support of Mamadou Diouf, Karen Barkley, and Katherine Ewing. Above all I owe much to the discussions, during many years, with the students who took my seminars on Islamic philosophy first at Cheikh Anta Diop University in Dakar, then at Northwestern, and now at Columbia.

INTRODUCTION

This book had as its title, literally translated from its original French, *How to Philosophize in Islam?* The subtitle adopted here, *Muslim Philosophers in Conversation with the Western Tradition*, describes in a more explicit way its object.[1] It is certainly inscribed in the rich literature on the history of philosophy in the Islamic world. It comes for a great part from my teaching, during many years, of a seminar on that topic and many reference works in the field bear precisely such a title: *History of Islamic Philosophy*.[2] But from that history a selection is made here, as certain particular questions are spotlighted along with the authors that can help examine them: How did the encounter between Islam and philosophy happen? Does religion need philosophy? What are the implications of the Arabic language becoming philosophical as it received translations from Greek texts? What does it mean to interpret philosophically a religious narrative? Can the religion coexist with philosophical rationalism? Is mysticism in contradiction with rationalism? What does it mean to be human? What is the responsibility of the human being vis-à-vis nature? Is there such a thing as an "Islamic" State or are Muslims free to invent the political institutions that correspond to the demands of their time and allow them to live in open, democratic societies?

Obviously such questions are not simply about the *history* of philosophy; they also speak to our *present* time and converge toward the very project of the chapters that address them: to contribute to the reconstruction, for today, of a critical spirit, of a spirit of movement and pluralism as manifested in the intellectual and spiritual tradition of Islam.

Those questions are posed and examined through the reading of texts by different Muslim philosophers of the classical period, from the ninth century to the twelfth, but also of the modern period, the nineteenth century and twentieth.

Thus, after an introductory chapter presenting a brief history of the constitution of what became a tradition of philosophy in the Muslim world, the second evokes the figure of theologian and grammarian Abū Sa'īd Al-Sīrāfī, who engaged in 922 in a famous intellectual joust with philosopher and logician Abū Bishr Mattā about the universality of Aristotelian logic. Is there such a thing as a grammar of reasoning in general or shouldn't we consider that Aristotle's categories are simply the categories of his own Greek language, every other language, especially Arabic, having its own logic? That debate has often been evoked in different histories of Islamic philosophy. It is of interest to examine the echo it found in the twentieth century in the reflections of Rwandan philosopher Alexis Kagamé (1912–81) or French linguist Émile Benveniste (1902–76), who, in 1956 and 1958 respectively, examined what Aristotle's logical categories owe to Greek grammar and linguistic categories.[3]

Philosopher Abū 'Ali Ibn Sīnā (c. 980–1037), also known as Avicenna, is presented here, in chapter 3, through a text attributed to him in which he carries out a systematic *translation*, into the language of philosophy, of a narrative central to the Muslim imaginary, which is the Ascent of the prophet Muhammad. The text offers a model of what a philosophical reading of a religious text means.

The figure of Abū Hamīd al-Ghazālī (1058–1111) is evoked in two chapters of the book (chapter 4 and chapter 10) where he presents two different faces. First he offers the visage of a theologian and a mystic who attacks philosophers, accusing them of being heretics because of excessive rationalism: here Ghazālī speaks on behalf of what he considers the one sect destined for salvation among all the other interpretations of Islam that existed in the troubled times when he lived. In the conclusion, on the contrary, we see his other face as a modern philosopher and an eloquent and committed advocate for pluralism, not only of Islamic sects, but also of religions more generally. Nobody expresses better than this Janus of Islam the tension that can exist between closure and an ideal of openness, as it is still at work, today, in the Muslim world.

It was important to evoke, in chapter 5, the figure of the philosopher from Andalusia Abū Bakr Ibn Tufayl (c. 1105–85), whose main work, the philosophical novel *Hayy Ibn Yaqzān*, can be read as a lesson in ecological philosophy: it demonstrates why the human being, when fully understanding who she is and who she has to become, may think of herself not as "master and possessor" (Descartes) of a nature considered resources to be exploited, but as endowed with the responsibility of acting as its steward and the guarantor of its integrity.

Abū Walīd Ibn Rushd (1126–98), known as Averroes, represents the response to Ghazālī's attacks on philosophers. He embodies faith in reason and in the necessity to interpret the religious text under its light. Chapter 6 is devoted to an example of a rationalist reading of the Quranic text and more generally to his contention that it is religion itself that demands rational interpretation and the development of philosophy.

The demand for the Muslim world to develop again philosophy is central to the works of reformist Islamic thinkers eager to see the world of Islam reanimate and rejuvenate the spirit of openness and inquiry that allows for the critical reappraisal of its own intellectual tradition and the reappropriation of the ethos of modernity. In the chapters 7, 8, and 9, figures of reformist philosophers are presented with the questions they help discuss. Jamāl ad-Dīn al-Afghānī (1838–97), in chapter 7, and Muhammad Abduh (1849–1905), in chapter 8, have thus insisted on the demand that systems of education in Muslim societies undergo a deep reform as the only way out of sclerosis, by making room for a teaching of philosophy that, more than technology, is the true spirit of modernity. Also in chapter 8, Ameer Ali (1849–1928) and Ali Abdel Razek, meditating on the lessons to be drawn, in the present, and for the future, from the history of Islam, call Muslim societies to the responsibility and the task of deriving from the premise that each age requires responses that are new, appropriate, and creative and needs to pull out of what Muhammad Iqbal (1877–1938) has called the "false respect of the past."

Muhammad Iqbal's thought, to which the next chapter is devoted, is indeed, directly or indirectly, at the heart of this book. His teaching that, because it is the very definition of life to be constant newness, religion cannot be in dogmatic tension against time, becoming, and pluralism is the very inspiration of these reflections on philosophy in the Islamic world.

It was important for me to end the book, in its conclusion, on the figure of a Muslim sage from Mali, Tierno Bokar Salif Tall (c. 1875–1939), who gives such a concrete, human—so human—face to a philosophy of pluralism, openness, and tolerance. His teaching, in a word, was that God loves all beings, including those some call "infidels." Because His name is *Rahmān*, the Merciful.

OPEN TO REASON

1

AND HOW TO NOT PHILOSOPHIZE?

In the year 632 of our common era, Muhammad died in Medina at the age of sixty-two. He had become a prophet at the age of forty, when he declared that, being charged with propagating faith in a single God, he was the carrier of a message, the Qur'an, God's own word that was revealed to him. Bit by bit, in spite of persecution, ostracism, forced exile, and military attacks that all aimed to annihilate it, out of this Word a religion, Islam, was born, which aimed to undo the old tribal relations and install in their place a community based on radically different rules of individual and collective life. The Qur'an was understood to be the inspiration from which this community was born and developed, but the words revealed by Muhammad—in which God declared who He was, the meaning of His creation, and the origin and destiny of humanity—did not constitute a treatise of government or a juridical system. A glance at the presentation of the Quranic text shows this clearly: its 6,236 verses (or 6,219, according to another division) treating various themes, grouped in 114 chapters arranged by length, were assembled by the Prophet's close companions—in these verses that pass from narration to exhortation, from legislative speech to mystical comparisons, can be found neither treatise nor system. In addition, the Quranic text, which is often self-referential, declares that certain of its passages contain nothing explicit for those who would like to read them simply by the letter, but are there to provoke thought among "people of understanding."[1]

While at the head of the first Muslim community, the group of companions he had formed around himself, Muhammad brought prophetic illumination to questions that were brought to him. Over twenty-three years the revelation came to him in fragments, often in verses that responded to particular circumstances; he clarified their meaning while also speaking universally beyond those circumstances. How should such and such a Quranic passage be understood? one companion would ask. He would provide clarification. What should be done in such and such a circumstance? another would ask. He would respond. But he had forbidden the posing of questions of pure speculation, those raised from imagined and fabricated situations in a casuistry that, taking itself as its own object, disconnects itself from the very movement of life through which real questions arise. This interdiction had a clear meaning: the future must be left open; possibilities should not be imagined only to have their meaning immediately saturated and closed off.

The Prophet's death marked the anxious experience of this openness. Certainly, his declarations had been collected, along with the acts he had performed in certain circumstances; together these made up his tradition or custom, his *sunna*, as is said in Arabic. If a decision, interpretation, or piece of advice could be validated through recourse to a prophetic saying (*hadith*), it was as if the Prophet had spoken. But for this, one such saying would need to be found that was applicable to the case in question, and such a hadith would need to be established as authentic. (When the science of traditions or hadith was formed later, the questions used to decide to what degree a hadith is or is not firmly established were along these lines: What is the chain of oral transmission for this hadith? Is it credible? To what extent?) But what if there was not one? Or if several sayings, each applicable to the situation under consideration, led in different directions? The goal was to remain faithful to the Prophet's message by continuing his *sunna*, his custom, in order to avoid any innovation that might deviate from the path he had traced. But when life itself is continuous innovation, how should fidelity be understood? What does it call for, in the ceaselessly renewed circumstances that life's movement brings?

The Prophet had not yet been buried before the chasm of options that his death opened up imposed its terrifying experience onto the community he had put together around the Qur'an and his own person. In his last days, while ill, he had asked his friend and faithful companion Abu Bakr to lead the collective prayers: In doing this, had he intended to indicate him as his successor (*khalif*) at the head of the new nation? Or instead, did the many examples of his affection for his cousin, adoptive son, and son-in-law, Ali, show that the role of Imam (guide) of the faithful should fall to this latter and his descendants, the children of the Prophet's youngest daughter Fatima? The question of who should lead the Islamic community opposed those who declared themselves the partisans of Ali, *Shi'a* Ali or *Shi'ites*, to those who decided to place at their head first Abū Bakr (from 632 to 634), then Umar (from 634 to 644), another friend and companion of the Prophet, then Uthmān (from 644 until his assassination in 656), another companion and his son-in-law twice over, and finally Ali himself (from Uthmān's death until his own assassination in 662). Those who later would maintain that these first four caliphs of Islam were all "rightly guided" (*rāshidūn*) in the path of the Prophet's *sunna* would give themselves the name *Sunnis*. The major schism in Islam, between Sunni majority and Shi'a minority, was therefore created over a political question, which would also become a theological question: that of the "commander of the faithful." And nevertheless each party believed the question to be resolved through fidelity to the Prophet and the message he had brought. All parties were confident that such a decision could be considered above discussion, controversy, and speculation, that it could, in other words, be mechanically inferred from the Qur'an and the Tradition. But when the meaning of fidelity itself proves to be a matter of speculation, how not to philosophize?

Who should govern? What does it mean to lead a community as the successor of a prophet, a Legislator who spoke in the name of God? Philosophical reflection would need to take up such questions. We can encounter our own present-day problems by pushing this reflection further, drawing out the consequences of the Legislator having left open the question "Who should govern?" Did this not make it an exclusively human affair, one to be treated as such in all its aspects? If the first Muslim community chose its first four caliphs by four different procedures—the first by consensus among a central group of companions, the second by the will of the first, the third chosen by "Grand Electors" designated by his predecessor, and the last one practically forced to accept the role of caliph due to times of sedition and civil war—the lesson can be drawn that Muslim societies are free to invent their states and the manner of choosing their representatives. So much, then, for the idea that in Islam religion and state cannot be separated, or that democracy cannot be imagined as a political regime in Muslim societies.

Other questions also came to be posed concerning the understanding of the Quranic text itself, and along with these the question of predestination or of free will. Does the human being act according to its own total free will or, on the contrary, is she determined and therefore predestined by God to go in one direction rather than another? "I did it not of my own accord," Khidr explained to Moses, when just before leaving him he revealed the meaning of acts that to Moses had seemed totally incomprehensible, immoral, or contrary to good sense.[2] Only someone who could take on God's point of view, seeing the consequences of an action in the most distant future, could grasp how everything is preordained in the infinity of divine wisdom. But on the other hand, the way the Qur'an narrates the initial appearance of the human being seems to recognize that he is the depositary of a treasure he alone can manifest: freedom. The possibility that frightened the angels—that through the arrival of humanity disorder and violence would be introduced into creation[3]—is the sign that with Adam and Eve arrived the power to say no, to do otherwise, to make negativity exist within the fullness of being. This is also why, preceding and announcing it like its shadow, the freedom of the human creature provided the occasion for Satan/Iblīs to discover his capacity for revolt and pay the price for his refusal to bow down before another than God, a command he saw as humiliation, with his demotion and his becoming "the stoned one" (rajīm). But the corollary of the human freedom to say no is its capacity to know the names by which God loves to be called, when he welcomes the repentance of the only being able to return to him, because it is the only one with the power to move away or turn aside through its own will. Free will or predestination: this will not be decided by a contest of opposed citations. Many verses of the Qur'an lead in one direction; equally as many can be found that lead in another. Once again, it is necessary to philosophize.

If the human being enjoys free will in its actions and therefore has autonomous capacity, does this not limit God's *power*? But if the human does not have the capacity to act according to its own free will, does this not void God's *justice* of any meaning? What sense would there be in recompensing or punishing, in this world or the other, someone who is nothing but an irresponsible marionette? Those who held the events and actions that happen in the world to be predetermined, who saw in them constraint (*jabr*) at work, made up the current of thought known as Jabirite, that is to say, "believers in determinism." After seditions, civil wars, and schisms, and with the advent of the Umayyad dynasty (who would make the caliphate a hereditary position from 662 to 750 CE) after the death of the fourth caliph, Ali, it could be morally convenient to declare that, if fratricidal combat had broken out between the Prophet's closest associates, this was because fate had determined the course of things and set them against one another. In addition, a power whose ability to maintain itself owed more to its capacity to maintain order and peace than to its unjustified dynastic principle took an interest in encouraging fatalism and belief in predestination. The Umayyads encouraged interpretations tending toward a conservative belief that everything is already written: politics, as always, was at play in philosophical speculation. Opposed to the *jabirites*, theses that held that human capacity for action (*qadr*) was essential to the meaning of justice would come to be called *qadirite*. We should not be surprised to see that under the Abbasid dynasty (from 750 to 1258), which overthrew the Umayyads through a movement of revolt, qadirite theses, affirming free will, were supported by the political powers, and that certain representatives of the Abbasid dynasty, as we will see, made them an element of official doctrine.

Along with the question of predestination or free will, thinkers faced that of the relation of the divine essence to the predicates attributed to it in the Qur'an. Clearly anthropomorphic ways of speaking of God presented a problem, for instance, passages that mention his "face," his "hand," or the fact that he is "seated on the Throne." The "hand" could be interpreted, for example, as signifying "power" and the "face" as signifying "the very being," and "sitting on the Throne" could be considered an expression of the majesty of the Lord of the worlds. But there is more to the question than the possibility of such "translations": it has to do with the very meaning of the unity of God. From this point of view, the anthropomorphism of expressions like "the face" or "the hand" of God, along with other seemingly more comprehensible attributes like "omniscient," "all-hearing," "all-seeing," "the living," "the manifest," "the hidden," and so on, introduces multiplicity into unity. Is not to understand this unity to comprehend that no single attribute is sufficient to describe the invisible and transcendent divine essence? Is there another way to speak of God apart from this negative one, consisting in saying what he is not? But in this case, how to make sense of all these attributes, since it is the Qur'an itself that declares them "the most beautiful names" of God? One possible response is to say that these are *ways of speaking* of God that in no way can touch his *way of being one.* Here the text would have spoken in the language of humans, while the divine unity is to be thought beyond such a language: the Jewish philosopher Maimonides, whose thought also drew on this speculative Islamic tradition, would later say, repeating the Talmud, that the Torah speaks the language of the children of Adam. In other words, God created a Word for humans, in language accessible to their reason, and invited them to interpret it and apply to it their full capacity of free examination. He *created* it: this would then mean that this Word, along with the other attributes, is not associated with him in a way that would make it partake in His eternity.

In one of the many verses where it refers to itself, the Qur'an declares: "A Revelation from the All-Merciful, Compassionate to each! Behold a Book whose verses are made distinct, an Arabic Qur'an to a people who have knowledge" (41:2–3).[4] An "Arabic Qur'an"? There are two ways to understand this expression. The first takes it as exalting the Arabic language, the language of Revelation, sacred because it was chosen out of all the others to speak the Word of God, chosen because it is sacred. The other, which conforms more to what the Qur'an itself says, understands the expression this way: God has chosen a human language, simply human, distinguished in its humanity by nothing in particular, to carry his Word, to make his Qur'an speak. To make this clearer, elsewhere He reminds us that He has honored all the children of Adam by sending them, wherever they are found, a messenger who speaks like them: "We sent no Messenger except with the language of his people, that he may enlighten them" (14:4). If there is, then, a language of the Qur'an, there is no language of Islam—or else all human languages are. It is often said that the Qur'an has a special, internal relationship to the Arabic language in which it was revealed that renders it untranslatable. But either this is a simple truism—nothing is truly translatable from one language to another—or else it is obscurantism: Why would the Revelation address itself to humans if at the same time it does not speak to them?

Predetermination, the meaning of human responsibility, the relation of attributes to the divine essence, the Qur'an as created or uncreated: the different answers given to each of these questions would also generate different schools of philosophical thought born from the need to understand the word (*kalām*) of God. The "science of the word," in Arabic *'ilm al-kalām* or simply *kalām*, was born as a discipline concerned with these questions. This discipline stood apart from and could not be easily incorporated into the landscape of the "sciences" said to be "religious," which held closely to the Quranic message. Among these was the science of the most literal possible commentary of the Qur'an (*tafsīr*); it rested on the linguistic sciences needed for the full comprehension of the text as it had been revealed: Arabic grammar and rhetoric. In addition, because the Muslim community born from the Quranic revelation was created in opposition to the tribal laws that had previously ruled relations of power (or between men and women), defined crime and punishment, and so on, the science of Muslim jurisprudence (called *fiqh*) developed to accompany the evolution of the community. It relies, in addition to the Qur'an, on the sayings attributed to the Prophet and the actions that he took in different circumstances: so a science of hadith, of the oral traditions concerning the sayings and actions of the Prophet, and their consequences, became an essential foundation of the "religious sciences."

Kalām could only be located at the edges of these "religious sciences." From one viewpoint, its declared object is the defense of the doctrines of the faith; it is, according to the definition given by the celebrated Ibn Khaldūn (d. 1404), "the science that involves arguing with rational proofs in defense of the articles of faith and refuting innovators who deviate from the beliefs of early Muslims and Muslim orthodoxy." But from another viewpoint, because its approach to religious matters consists in having reason weigh revelation in its scales, *kalām* itself potentially produces "innovations" that consist in judging rationally more than in forcing its way of seeing to conform to what is supposed to be that of "the first Muslims."

To defend the articles of faith by reason above all is also to *reconstruct* them according to this reason and therefore, in the eyes of those for whom fidelity is only in the repetition of the identical, to fall into rationalism. The fear that reason, taking itself as its own goal, will turn itself into eristics, whose goal is to rationally defeat one's adversaries' arguments, is expressed in an anecdote about the founder of one of the central schools of jurisprudence in Islam, Abū Hanīfa (d. 767). When he forbade his son from taking part in *kalām* debates, the son was shocked to be forbidden from a path in which his father was himself a master. Abū Hanīfa gave this reply: "When we were engaged in this, we all kept silent out of fear of seeing our interlocutor fall into error; but as for you, each of you is engaged in these discussions with the hope of seeing his companion slip and fall into unbelief. Whoever wishes this falls into the same trap himself."

Fear of reason, and fear that its use leads to slipping and falling into unbelief: those who fear nothing more than reason given over to its own power, free and questioning thought, are quick to denounce speculation that seems to have "seceded from dogmatic thought."[5] "Secession," *i'tazala* in Arabic, gave its name to the theologians who became known as *mu'tazilites*, that is to say, literally, "those who are separated." It is also said, to explain the origin of the name, that Hassan al-Basri (d. 728), who was a founder of both theological reflection in Islam and a certain systematization of Sufism or Islamic mysticism, declared of his rationalist and dissident students: "You have separated yourselves from us." The Mu'tazilites for their part referred to themselves by their philosophical positions as "partisans of unity and justice," that is to say, divine unity uncompromised by the multiplicity of attributes, and the justice of God as applicable only to individuals free in their actions.

We can speak, then, of a fear of reason. But what of a situation where rationalism puts itself in the position of demanding that everyone conform to its demands, ready to reign, if needed, by terror? Would it be an absolute contradiction to see reason choosing to win hearts and minds by force? This was what occurred when the political powers, particularly during the twenty years of the reign of the caliph al-Ma'mun (from 813 to 833), decided to impose Mu'tazilite rational—that is to say, rationalistic—theology as official doctrine. The characteristic event of this rationalist inquisition—an oxymoron known in the intellectual history of the Muslim word by the name *mihna*—was the imprisonment under al-Ma'mun of the jurist Aḥmad ibn Ḥanbal, who was accused of a criminal stubbornness in refusing the rational "Truth" of the created Qur'an, which was declared an official article of faith by the caliph in 817, four years after he came to power. Remaining stoic under torture, the jurist, who would be liberated and rehabilitated under al-Ma'mun's successor, thus became the symbol of the human spirit's capacity to resist oppressive dogmatism, which in this case happened to be that of reason.

Mu'tazilite rational philosophy would be associated, after this period, with oppression and the danger of irreligion: a proverb declared that he who reasons too much and too freely becomes an unbeliever. Still today, the rejection of Mu'tazilism and its excesses is evoked to dismiss academic programs in critical thought. Literalism holds pride of place in certain Muslim countries, where the authorities, claiming fidelity to the "Ancients," narrowly conceived of as the identical repetition of their supposed way of thinking and acting, consequently forbid not only the teaching of philosophy but also that of *kalām*; this is the case in Saudi Arabia. What is said of the *hand*, the *face*, or the *throne* of God must be accepted, say the literalists, "without asking 'why,'" as prescribed by Aḥmad ibn Ḥanbal, hero of resistance to Mu'tazilite power. Despite this, history shows that the rejection of Mu'tazilism did not necessarily mean the rejection of rational theological speculation, since this, once again, is inevitable: because the revelation speaks to those who are human and think, there is never a zero degree of interpretation, and literalism is merely *one* reading, though it pretends not to be.

At the start of the tenth century, a reaction would come from the very heart of the Mu'tazilite school, called *ash'arite*, after Hassan al-Ash'arī (approx. 873–941), who founded this *kalām* in response to rationalist excesses. A Mu'tazilite until the age of forty, he dramatically broke with his master and the doctrine he had professed until then by declaring from the heights of the lectern in the Mosque of Baghdad: "Those who know me know who I am, and those who do not know me, let them know that I am Abū Ḥassan al-Ash'arī, and that I used to profess that the Qur'an was created, that human eyes would never see God and that creatures create their actions themselves Alas! I repent of having been a Mu'tazilite. I renounce these opinions and I take on the task of refuting the Mu'tazilites, exposing their childishness and turpitude."[6]

At least this is how tradition has chosen to give a dramatic flair to the rupture out of which Ash'arite theology was born. Note the symbolic value of the age of forty, considered the age of prophecy. It is said, as well, that al- Ash'arī took the decision to give his recantation a public resonance after a dream in which he saw the Prophet in person. Whatever the case, what is certain is that he judged Mu'tazilism insufficient on the precise theological problem of reconciling God's justice (the strict retribution of actions according to their nature) and his mercy (the capacity to erase evil actions, or to increase the value of good ones). Different stories have dramatized this intellectual and religious disagreement. For instance, al-Ash'arī is said to have one day "stumped" al-Jubba'i (d. 915), his master up until then, with this puzzle: There are three brothers, all of whom received the same education. At death, the first one is recompensed for his good deeds and goes to paradise; the second, who was a sinner, is punished and finds himself in hell; the third, who died at a young age without gaining knowledge of good and evil, resides in limbo. Here, it seems, the algebra of divine justice as understood by Mu'tazilism is respected. But suppose, proposed al-Ash'arī, that the third brother asks God: "Why did you not allow me to live so that I could do good like my brother?" His brother, the damned, then raises the stakes: "Why did you not make me die at a young age and spare me the life that led me to hell?" The story tells that al-Jubba'i, perplexed, could not respond to his disciple, who then took leave of him.

Ash'arism is first a spiritual, and then an intellectual, insurrection against the idea of a God entirely of reason, ultimately abstract, and incomprehensible in his transcendent transparency. It is a demand for a personal God, with attributes by which we can call him, since he has given us his names, the most beautiful ones, in his Book; it is a call for a God toward whom there is a sense in addressing prayers for small and great things, for escape from inevitability, and who can, responding to one shed tear, erase all the sins of a dissolute existence—without room for a "why?" Reason is not dismissed—to the contrary, Ash'arite *kalām* wants reason to indicate the route at whose finely narrowed end can rise, authentic and pure, the prayer born from perplexity that leads to the encounter with God.

To simplify, let us say that Ash'arism is a reaction against the excesses of rationalism; and let us further simplify by adding that, beyond the differences between the two theologies, Mu'tazilism and Ash'arism represent two *attitudes* or *spirits* that continuously, in ever-renewed forms, fight over the field of Islamic thought. Mu'tazilism groups together extremely diverse theologies, it is true, but in all of them can be seen a shared spirit, one that might be called philosophical, of the audacity of reason, opposed to the spirit of Ash'arism, which cares to hold society together by not exposing it to speculative excesses that might lead to a separation of elites from the people as well as to divisions within those elites. Philosophy, in Islam, is allied with the Mu'tazilite spirit, while, as we will see, Ash'arism inspired the most celebrated condemnation of philosophy, by al-Ghazālī in the eleventh century.

But more than a historically dated school, Mu'tazilism is the possibility and necessity, in Islam, of philosophy. Today, when, to cite the work of the Indian poet-philosopher Muhammad Iqbal (1877–1938), the necessity of *reconstructing religious thought in Islam* imposes itself, the Mu'tazilite spirit resurfaces, and is found in certain reformist thinkers like the Egyptian Muhammad Abduh

(d. 1905) or the Indian Ameer Ali (d. 1928), or in those who, at present, continue the task of bringing the modernity that Islam carries to light by uncovering possibilities of reform internal to the religion.

2

HOW A LANGUAGE BECOMES PHILOSOPHICAL

The caliph al-Ma'mun had a dream. From across the barrier of centuries, Aristotle appeared to him. Al-Ma'mun was an Arab; in his dream the Greek philosopher took the form of a blond and blue-eyed man. The two had this conversation: "I asked him: 'Who are you?' He replied: 'I am Aristotle.' I was glad to hear this, and said to him: 'O master, let me question you.' He said to me: 'Ask.' I asked him: 'What is the good?' He responded: 'What is good according to reason.' I said to him, 'And then?' He replied: 'What is good according to revelation.' I said to him, 'And then?' He replied: 'What is good in the eyes of all.' I said to him: 'And then?' He replied 'After that there is no "and then."' . . . I said to him: 'Tell me something else.' He said: 'Let whoever counsels you well concerning gold be like gold to you. And you must acknowledge One God.'"[1]

As mentioned earlier, al-Ma'mun held Mu'tazilite opinions in theology. It was natural for Aristotle, in his imagination, to begin by saying that truth must appear to reason before it is established by revelation. After all, if God wishes for his Word to be transmitted to the children of Adam, first of all he must have created in them the capacity to understand, which is reason. It was evident, too, to both the Greek philosopher and his interlocutor that common opinion would come afterward. But where did this image of Aristotle, a monotheist who confirmed the caliph's rationalist positions, come from? Jean Jolivet has perceptively said that this dream offered the chance to at once represent and resolve the tension between the Muslim intellectual world's desire to open itself up to Greek thought and its hesitation in pursuing a "wisdom" other than the necessarily complete and sufficient one of the Quranic revelation.[2]

If, then, Aristotle himself advises turning toward the One God, the matter is settled; and as he speaks literally and figuratively of gold, he and his philosophy can be held as precious as this metal. This is how the caliph understood the divine message carried by this inspired dream, and he took the decision to create an institution wholly dedicated to the philosophical sciences where the greatest scholars would devote themselves to translating the works of Greek thought into Arabic. The year 832, when the "House of Widsom" (*bayt al-hikma*) was built, marked the birth of a philosophical tradition from the encounter of Greek thought and the universe of Islam, known by the name of *falsafa*, an Arabization of the Greek *philosophia*. One clarification should be made, however: the project of translating philosophical work into Arabic had not waited for the solemn act of the House of Wisdom's construction. Works of Greek science, including Ptolemy's *Almagest* and Aristotle's *Logic*, had been translated since the end of the eighth century. The world of scholarship, happily, does not wait for a pronouncement from political power to carry out the movement of openness that is in its nature.

Nonetheless, it is undeniable that al-Ma'mun's project gave a decisive push toward the Muslim world's appropriation of Greek philosophy, while also giving credence to the idea of an eternal wisdom (*philosophia perennis*), which humanity never lacks, even in the absence of revelation, since people everywhere think, love, know themselves mortal, and look at the skies. Thanks to "divine" men, like "the divine Plato," this wisdom is there and it is the duty of each to appropriate it for themselves. The Prophet himself declared that "the word of wisdom is the lost property of the believer; wherever he finds it, he has a right to it." The House of Wisdom, at root, was a monument set up to the idea of a perennial human wisdom uniquely able to illuminate even divine revelations in order to make them better understood. Translators, copyists, and bookbinders, all given stipends by the caliph himself, worked to make this idea a reality. The institution was also a hymn to confessional pluralism: the first translators who directed the House were Christians, as it had been the Nestorian and Jacobite schools of Christian thought that had preserved the essentials of the Aristotelian heritage in the monasteries of Syria and Iraq. "Philosophy in the lands of Islam" has, in fact, always been "a Muslim history, it goes without saying, but also a Christian and a Jewish history."[3]

Philosophy in the lands of Islam is a history of meetings: Greek philosophy with Islamic themes; Syriac and Greek with Arabic; theological-philosophical traditions interlaced in such a way that any history of Medieval philosophy that tries to follow the single thread of Christian Latin philosophy, as is often the case, will be truncated and incomplete. Alain de Libera, who has given us a restored image of Medieval philosophy as a proliferation of encounters and intermingled traditions, writes: "Philosophy in the lands of Islam is not the philosophy of Muslims, but the history of the philosophies that Muslims produced or helped produce after the conquest: pagan, Christian, Muslim, Jewish; Muslim philosophy by religious figures, 'secular' philosophy by philosophers; Oriental and Occidental philosophies, Mediterranean or continental, Arab or non-Arab, Persian philosophies and Turkish philosophies."[4]

The first translations, by Nestorian masters, were from Syriac texts through which Greek philosophy was studied in the monasteries. The movement of translation posed new philosophical problems to Muslim thought, such as the meaning of creation in opposition to the idea of the eternity of the world found in Proclus, to give one example. It would also perform what had already happened to Latin in the time of Cicero: making Arabic a philosophical language. Toward that end, new words were needed: for instance, out of *kayfa*, meaning "how" in Arabic, the world *kayfiyya* was formed, producing a substantive through the addition of the suffix -*iyyah*, to render "quiddity." One can note, too, that the philosophical concept of the "quiddity" of a thing, that is to say, what it is, its "quality," was formed on the same model, beginning from the Latin *quid* ("which") and the suffix -*itas*, -*ity* in English, or -*ité* in French. Philosophizing in Latin, or in Arabic—there is nothing in the essence of philosophy that demands that it speak Greek, or that it be born in that language. Cicero wrote philosophical texts against the skepticism of those who thought that philosophy was only suited to Greek: "Why," he asked, "can they not bear the idiom of their country when discussing the most serious subjects?"[5] For their part, the Arabic translators of what Cicero called "this ancient philosophy whose origin is in Socrates" had to confront those who could not bear for "the idiom of their country" to be touched by the hybridization that translation inevitably creates. And to translate "ancient philosophy" into Arabic, a Semitic language, posed different questions than translating it into Latin, which like Greek is an Indo-European language. Hence the neologisms forged by translators who also did some "violence" to usual modes of expression.

The *becoming-philosophical* of the Arabic language would also prompt a renewal of the quarrel over philosophy: to be for or against its inclusion among the sciences studied in the Islamic world was also to accept (or to oppose) the hybridization that translation imposes on a language that some thought should be left untouched, having been designated "pure" by its receiving the Quranic revelation. In 932, a century after the foundation of the House of Wisdom, a famous public controversy opposed a representative of the Hellenizing philosophers, Abū Bishr Mattā, to a representative of the Arabic "grammarians," the guardians of the integrity of the language. Abū Saʿīd al-Sīrāfī was their champion in the dispute that played out in the court of the Seljuk Vizir Ibn al-Furāt. The philosopher and man of letters Abū Ḥayyān al-Tawḥīdī (d. 1023) provided an account of the encounter, which he was said to have received from Sīrāfī himself. He was known, among other things, for providing abridgments of many theological and philosophical controversies of his day, in cultural circles that displayed a remarkable openness of spirit. The intellectual elite that debated in these circles was characterized by a tolerant attitude that allowed peaceful dialogue between Muslims and Christians or Jews, Sunnis and Shi'ites, Mu'tazilites and Asharites, in an atmosphere of openness to difference that Abu Hayyān al-Tawḥīdī vividly describes.[6]

But the debate between Sirāfī and Mattā was hardly marked by a spirit of openness or respectful listening. To the contrary, the grammarian Sirāfī draped himself, aggressively and with animosity, in the garb of a guardian of the Arabic language against the pretensions of logic and Greek philosophy to seek welcome and hospitality there. There was also a confessional animosity: Mattā, a philosopher and a Christian, appeared to his adversary as a perfect illustration of what that foreign "wisdom" threatened to impose on the language God chose to carry his Word. Sirāfī's speech is perpetual violence: he poses to Mattā linguistic puzzles, he acerbically emphasizes his linguistic faults, he interrupts him and, ultimately, leaves no space for him to develop his thoughts because he limits him to responding directly to questions. Behind the philosopher's attempts to express himself clearly, one can make out the thesis that there are universal truths transcending the differences of culture and language, that translation, carried out according to the rules of this difficult art, is perfectly capable of capturing truths first expressed in a given language into another idiom, and that this fact is also what defines truth: as long as the meanings are perfectly intelligible, translation, necessarily, will preserve them as such.

In this era of translation and appropriation, another important reflection was written on what it might mean to transpose the ways of speaking and the knowledge of one culture into another, from one language into another. Al-Jāhiz (d. 869), one of the most prolific and talented of Arabic prose writers, a Mu'tazilite theologian among other things, made it to the capital, Baghdad, during the reign of the caliph al-Ma'mun, and wrote pages of a striking "modernity" on the demands of translation and on its very possibility. This author, an African, or an "Ethiopian" as the Ancients would say, was one of the greatest connoisseurs of the Arabic language. In terms that are not without resemblance to Sirāfī's, he insisted on the idea that each language has its own genius and ways of speaking that are not transposable into another, and that a back-and-forth between two languages also always provokes hybridization, one of the idioms "harming the other."[7] To this he added practical considerations as to the state and quality of the manuscripts collected for translation.

But let us return to Mattā and to the heart of his argument. Intelligibles, he said to Sirāfī, are the same for all men, in all languages, and he asked him: "Do you not see that four and four make eight for all nations, and that it is the same with everything similar?"[8] All truth that is rational, and therefore "similar to four and four make eight," remains identical from one language to another, and is perfectly translatable without loss. This claim performs a double objective. First, it responds to an ad hominem argument presented by Sirāfī, who mocked philosophers who did not know Greek themselves and whose knowledge of the philosophical text depended on a translation of the original work into Arabic by way of Syriac: consequently, they had access only to the translation of a translation and found themselves, Sirāfī supposed, doubly distanced from the truth. To this criticism, in fact applicable to the first period, where translations were made from Syriac texts and not from the original Greek, Mattā replied that distance from the original has no effect: truth, as the daughter of reason, which is everywhere identical to itself, remains intact after the double translation. Second, the claim becomes a profession of faith in the universal against Sirāfī's linguistic relativism, at the base of which is, ultimately, the thought that each language is a world in itself, with *its* specific logic: a grammar of thought in general, which the philosophers maintain exists, has no reality for him; all that is real are the different grammars of the different languages that humans speak. There is not, therefore, for Sirāfī, a science of logic, what Leibniz later would call a "philosophical grammar." There is a Greek logic as there is an Arabic logic, which is nothing other than the grammar of Arabic. In addition, he said to Mattā, "your" Aristotle, the one you pride yourselves in parroting, did nothing but present as universal logic, the grammar of thought in general, what in reality was only the grammar of his language. There is no reason, consequently, for those who speak a different language—and a fortiori the language of the Revelation—to bow down before the Stagirite's logic.

This debate, in truth, is of a stunning modernity. Sirāfī's position would find a distant echo in Émile Benveniste's thesis that the "categories of thought" Aristotle lists are nothing but the "categories of [the Greek] language."[9] When the ninth-century grammarian opposes the universalism of the logician Mattā with the claim that "one only arrives at intelligible ends and exact significations through language,"[10] one is struck by how much this agrees with Benveniste's remark that "no matter how abstract or specialized the operations of thought may be, they receive expression in language."[11] Can we then, Benveniste asks (and this, eleven centuries earlier, is the question Sirāfī posed), admit universal categories of thought that are not those of any particular language? He replies, in substance, after studying the famous table established by Aristotle, that the categories claimed to be universal "turn out to be transposed from categories of language."[12]

The different ways of speaking about *being*? Those are simply so many modes of using the word *to be* in Greek and, first of all, the possibility of making "being" an objectifiable notion, one that philosophical reflection can manipulate, analyze, and situate like any other concept. Take English, for example: one can pose the question "What is being?" in this language because it has the resource, by adding *-ing* to the verb *be*, of constructing *being*, and then posing questions with regard to it.[13] Can these questions (not to speak of their answers) be said to be universal when other languages without the same usage of the verb *to be* cannot even formulate them using the only ways of speaking they permit?

To illustrate his claim, Benveniste chooses to compare Greek to the Ewe language spoken in Togo and Ghana, in which "the notion of 'to be,' or what we shall designate as such, is divided among several verbs."[14] This is more or less the same in Arabic, and this is why Sīrāfī, not only out of a narrow and closed spirit, perceived here a nontrivial aspect of what translation, from Greek to Syrian or to Arabic, implies for a logic that the *falāsifa* would like to be to the mind as syntax is to language. This is an analogy that is constantly repeated, found, for instance, in a manual of logic widely studied in the Maghreb and in centers of Islamic teaching that developed in Sub-Saharan Muslim Africa along with Islamization, *al-Sullam al-Murawwanaq* (*The Ornamented Ladder*), which dates from the first half of the fourteenth century.[15]

Let me conclude with two remarks. The first takes us back to the *becoming-philosophical* of languages. The example just mentioned, of the importance of the word *to be* to logical predication in Aristotle, explains why the philosopher-translators working in Arabic seemed to create, in the eyes of a scrupulous grammarian like Sīrāfī, an *other*, unacceptable language, with their neologisms and distorted formulations. To find an exact equivalent for the canonical form of the proposition in Aristotle, for example, "Socrates *is* walking," "S is P," with subject, copula, and predicate, they look for the same triptych and so write, in Arabic, the equivalent of "Socrates *is found walking*" or "Socrates, *he*, walking." Is this the imposition of the grammar/logic of one language on another? Sīrāfī certainly has grounds to argue this from his point of view as guardian of the *jus et norma loquendi*, the correct and usual modes of speaking.

In addition, from the point of view of the history of logic itself, the translators' insistence in making visible a *rabiṭa*, a copula, even though the Arabic language a priori does not allow writing "S is P," the canonical propositional form in Greek, has had importance. The copula they thus invented finds itself relieved of its ontological charge to become, in some way, no more than a *symbol* expressing the relation between concepts, a relation whose formal properties can be studied. When logic, with Leibniz and then with Boole, was expressed as a symbolic algebraic language, the transformation of the copula into a sign of equality echoed the methods of the translator-philosophers who constructed an equivalent in Arabic for the role of the verb *to be* in Aristotle's logic.

More generally, and this is the second remark, beyond the technical aspects (linguistic and logical) of the controversy, a dialectic of closure and opening is surely in play. Sīrāfī supports a closing-off from what Greece had thought, in its own idiom and for itself, according to him, in order to be better centered on a hermeneutics of the Revelation and its language, out of which will be born the only modes of knowledge—Grammar, Commentary, Theology, and above all Jurisprudence, which was promoted to the rank of queen of the sciences—that matter for the Islamic world. Mattā is on the side of an openness attested to by the hybridization that the Arabic language experienced by receiving Greek philosophy. This language then, in turn, would quickly become itself a language of philosophy in which Muslim philosophers as important for the universal history of ideas as Avicenna, al-Farābī, Ghazālī, Averroes, Ibn Tufayl, and others would write and think, along with Jewish philosophers like Saadia Gaon or Maimonides.

3

WHAT DOES IT MEAN FOR A PHILOSOPHY TO BE ISLAMIC?

In entering the Islamic world, then, philosophy kept its foreign, Greek name of *philosophia*, Arabized as *falsafa*, with *faylasūf* (or in the plural *falāsifa*) referring to a philosopher. This indicated clearly that it was a matter of a new discipline, one situated outside the borders of the "Islamic sciences" or "sciences of religion," while rational theology was perched with one foot inside and one outside. Should one then speak of "Islamic" philosophy? Or more generally, can philosophical questioning—which by its nature presupposes nothing without examination—be qualified, without contradiction, as Greek, Indian, Christian, or Islamic?

An "Islamization" of philosophy did occur, that is to say, an appropriation of Greek thought that was not only translated but also incorporated. Recall the caliph al-Ma'mun's dream: certainly, the blonde and blue-eyed portrait of Aristotle in his dream was a way for his unconscious to mark the Stagirite as a stranger; but this same unconscious equally transformed him into a strict monotheist, who spoke of Revelation's relation to reason and ended their dream interview by encouraging him to recognize only one God. Within the movement of the Islamization of philosophy and philosophers, one finds a proliferation of stories concerning a Socrates more resembling a Sufi master of wisdom than the mentor that Plato described in the dialogues he wrote down.

But beyond the local color given to the thoughts and thinkers of Greece, we can meaningfully speak of "Islamic philosophy" where the fundamental accounts of the religion were read and understood in the light of the teaching of Plato, Aristotle, Plotinus, and the like, for instance, concerning the meaning given to the human spirit's voyage toward the truth. A perfect illustration of this is the philosophical reconstruction Avicenna made of one of the most important traditions in Islam, the story of the Prophet Muhammad's ascent and encounter with God. This reconstruction carries the lesson that it is important to disengage from the marvelous, perhaps in order to better taste it, and to read the rational significations that it allegorizes.

The ascent properly speaking was preceded by a transport, one might say horizontal, from Mecca to Jerusalem, as described in the seventeenth chapter of the Qur'an, whose title is precisely "The Night Journey" (isrā) and whose first verse reads, "Glory be to Him Who carried His servant by night from the Sacred Mosque [masjid al-haram, in Mecca] to the Furthest Mosque [masjid al-aqsā, in Jerusalem], whose precincts We have blessed, to show him of Our wonders! He it is Who is All-Hearing, All-Seeing!" And chapter 53 speaks of the encounter at the end of the Ascent (Mi'rāj)—vertical—from Jerusalem as far as the "lotus-tree of the limit," where he saw, with a "gaze that did not waver," the "great wonders of his Lord."

Beyond these Quranic allusions, the tradition gives details of this ascension, in a rich literature that endlessly embroidered the story of the Prophet mounted on a fabulous steed and accompanied by the Archangel Gabriel going first to pray, with the prophets who had preceded him, in the Holy City of Jerusalem, and then climbing across the sky up to the limits of intelligibility: God himself. Not surprisingly, Muslim iconography over the years has found an inexhaustible source of inspiration in this story.

Here, in summary, is what the Muslim tradition says: While the Prophet was asleep in the courtyard of the Ka'aba in Mecca, the angel Gabriel came to wake him and presented him with a winged and pure white mount, something between a mule and a donkey, named al-Burāq. With Gabriel as guide, this mount carried him all the way to Jerusalem, where he encountered a group of prophets, including Abraham, Moses, and Jesus, whom he led in prayer. Al-Burāq then transported him from the rock of the Temple across the skies, where he again met the prophets he had seen in Jerusalem, this time transfigured into their celestial reality, seeing, for example, the legendary beauty of Joseph illuminated by divine splendor. After a vision of the marvels of Paradise came the vision of God and an audience with Him during which, along with certain Quranic passages, the Islamic duty of ritual prayer was revealed, to be performed a certain number of times each day; then, with Moses' instruction, he was able to bargain that number down from fifty to five in consideration of humans' all-too-human weakness.

This tradition speaks, undeniably, to the imagination; and it is in the language of images that intelligible realities must dress themselves in order to speak to all types of spirits, those who are touched by the marvelous as much as those who know how to grasp the unrepresentable indicated by the analogies in which it is presented. This was the task of the philosopher as conceived by the *falāsifa* from Avicenna to Ibn Tufāyl and to Averroes: to interpret, according to reason and its concepts, that which appears to be a story addressed to the imagination. Avicenna applied this principle in an essay he dedicated to the prophetic *Mi'rāj*, accordingly called *Mi'rāj Nama, The Book of the Ascent*. This is not one of Avicenna's major works, and specialists disagree on whether it should, in all certainty, be attributed to him; on this question (which Henry Corbin also raised), the appendix Peter Heath wrote to his English translation of the treatise is useful.[1] At any rate, the text is a perfect illustration of Avicenna's cosmology and psychology, and thus is at least Avicennian. The philosopher also invented other imaginative tales, on the model of the story of the ascension, in which he describes by means of allegories a voyage that is at once cosmic and unfolding within human psychology, across our faculties.

But first a word on Avicenna. His name, Latinized as Avicenna, was Abū ʿAli al-Husayn ibn ʿAbdallah ibn Sīnā. Of Persian origin, he was born in 980 near Bukhara, in today's Uzbekistan, and pursued his studies there. He was highly precocious, and proved to be a great master, at a very young age, of the "Islamic" sciences as well as the philosophical disciplines: mathematics, physics, logic, and metaphysics. His genius showed itself above all in medicine. His biography relates that he was hardly seventeen when he succeeded in healing a Muslim prince who lived in the city of a serious illness. This powerful man offered him favors in return, which included access to the important palace library, permitting him to become the encyclopedic spirit that he is remembered as. His story gave a lesson of perseverance to those searching for knowledge: he read and reread Aristotle's *Metaphysics* forty times before he stumbled on a little work by the *faylasūf* al-Farābī that gave him the key to its meaning. After the death of his patron and the end of the Samanid dynasty to which he belonged, Avicenna left Bukhara and traveled through Khorasan. He settled down in Hamadān, on the insistence of a prince who appointed him a minister so as to keep this great doctor close to him. In Hamadān Avicenna dedicated himself to the daunting task of writing commentaries on the works of Aristotle, while at the same time he drafted the celebrated *Canon of Medecine* that, in Salomon Munk's words, "contributed more than any of his other works to immortalizing his name and making him known even in Europe, where, for several centuries, the works of Ibn Sīnā were more or less considered the basis of medical studies."[2]

When this prince died, Ibn Sīnā did not get along well with his son and successor, and began contacting a rival prince from Isfahan; when this was discovered, he was thrown into prison. He took advantage of his imprisonment to write until, after several years, he was able to return to Isfahan, where he put himself in the service of a new prince. He lost the manuscripts of his work and his health as well while attending this prince's wars, and it was during a military expedition that he caught the intestinal infection from which he died. This man who lived in a troubled time, who was caught up in politics during an era of turbulence, and who lived a fairly nomadic life still wrote a body of work considerable in volume and in its importance for universal thought, writing at times in prison and at times literally on horseback. Called both "the Prince of Physicians" and "the Most Excellent Master" (referring to philosophy), he, it is said, did not refuse the pleasures of the table or other worldly pleasures during his adventurous life, and died a pious man in Hamadān, where the prince's wars had brought him, in 1037.

This master of Islamic peripateticism understood creation as a series of emanations through which divine thought produced a succession of Intelligences, identified with the Angels, from the First up to the Tenth, which is called the Active Intelligence and in some sense watches over each of us as a guardian angel, since it is what illuminates human intelligence and actualizes our capacity to understand intelligible realities, as light actualizes our capacity to see sensible things. In other terms, thanks to the effusion of the Active Intelligence, divine at its source, our intelligence is awakened from the passivity of its state of simple potentiality and so becomes active.

But we are not only intelligence. Just as the procession of Intellects in what we could call the superior world engendered both Souls and celestial spheres, they coexist within the human being, alongside the rational faculty that distinguishes it from other kingdoms, a vegetative faculty for nourishment and reproduction, a faculty of sensation, and an animal faculty of desiring. Since all this proceeds from God, it follows that everything desires to return to him. Everything in the human, the vegetal and the animal within him, along with the rational and the intelligent, is desire for the divine. This desire, Avicenna says in substance, is what woke the Prophet from his sleep on the Sacred Mosque's grounds and took him first to Jerusalem, the center of this world and therefore the door that opens onto the other world, and then across the skies, up to the threshold where one is in the very presence of God.

With regard to the important stage in Jerusalem, note that until after the Hegira, when that role shifted to Mecca, this city served as the point of orientation for Muslim prayer. But even then, as the later construction of the al-Aqsā Mosque materialized, this meeting point for the three monotheistic religions, Jerusalem, would never loose its status, in the eyes of the Muslims, as one of the manifestations of the Center.

The Book of Ascent opens with a warning. It addresses those who are seeking a rational explication, that is to say, a meaning founded on the very nature of things, of this journey. In other words: Lovers of the marvelous, abstain! This text is not addressed to you. Philosophizing relies on a strict discipline of the arcane that demands one be certain of addressing a mind well disposed toward that exercise and able to receive its truths and interpretations. In an image that translates the nature of this discipline of the arcane, Avicenna writes: "it is a fault to divulge secrets to a stranger."[3] On the other hand, he specifies that to refuse them to a person who potentially has the intelligence needed to receive them is also an error. This type of warning, which we will encounter again, is found frequently among philosophers as well as mystics (Sufis), and for the same reasons: literalist minds will be troubled and also infuriated by interpretations that connect the image to what it designates in a mode other than its relation to its literal meaning. But then, Sufis as well as philosophers are people of interpretation.

The chapter that immediately follows the introduction with that warning is a chapter of pure philosophy that does not mention the ascent itself. It is concerned first with human nature, made from the conjunction of two entities belonging to two different worlds: body and spirit.[4] In an image that evokes a comparison made by Plato in the Phaedrus, the union of spirit and body is compared to that of a rider and his mount. The body is animated by three types of soul: the natural, connected to the liver; the animal, linked to the heart; and the spiritual, which has its seat in the brain. The first two must serve the third one, which is specific to humanity, and to which belong rationality, wisdom, knowledge, and discernment. In this way humans are distinguished from one another, not by the natural constitution that they all share, but because of the domination that one soul, and function, or another exerts in their being. The ideal human being is one whose rational soul dominates and directs his different components toward the proper functioning of the whole, under the supervision of the intelligence also called the Holy Spirit, the most elevated faculty, which is turned upward and fixed on the Active Intelligence that feeds it intelligible realities.

The intelligence also has a practical dimension, through which the rational faculty can draw consequences, develop and make use of knowledge about sensible realities, to serve the interests of the rational animal. The rational soul differs from the intelligence but is not other: they are two names for the same reality. The soul is intelligence when it comes to grasping the intelligibles, and is discernment when it reasons and establishes distinctions, in the same way the faculty of perception of sensibles is smell when dealing with scents, vision with visible things, hearing with sound. It makes, then, great sense to say that human beings are the desire to realize themselves in the fullness that drives them toward the pleasure generated by the exercise of their highest faculty. Full pleasure, unmixed, is thus the one provided by the intelligizing of intelligible things, but the search for it—that is, the ascent toward oneself—does not stop at this first level. The intellect, which is at the center of our humanity, is also an openness to all of the Intelligences that emanate from God, thanks to the mediation of the Tenth, the Angel that watches over us from the nearest heaven and attracts us. When we come into contact with this or that Intelligence, this develops in us this or that knowledge or attitude. When we are united with the very first emanation, which Avicenna calls the First Guardian or Universal Intelligence, we fully become ourselves universal comprehension, and our intellect, seized by this Intelligence, becomes *prophetic*.

As has become clear, this presentation of the nature of the human as a desire to journey across the different heavens of the intelligence toward the full realization of the prophetic spirit is not an introduction or prologue to the rational explication of the ascent: it itself is this explication. The ascent is none other than the accession of the humans to what they are and have to be. The journey is cosmic because, first of all, it is microcosmic: if it takes place in the macrocosm, toward the beyond of this world and in the direction of God, this is because it takes place inside the human, in the direction of the self. In the chapter that follows, dedicated to a sentence-by-sentence commentary of the narrative of the prophetic ascent, Avicenna restores what is said in the language of images and symbols to the meanings that can be found for them in the Neoplatonic philosophical analysis of human psychology.

The prophet found himself in a state between waking and sleeping when everything began—this is because the silence of the senses, of the irascible faculty, and of imagination is the condition for the awakening of the spiritual faculty that is the desire for the truth.

Gabriel's arrival in angelic form—this is the manifestation of the faculty of the Holy Spirit, which illuminates human intellect and so transmits to it the commandment of God. As for the story, which Avicenna reproduces, of the angel embracing the Prophet, calling him his "brother" and kissing him between the eyes while enjoining him "O sleeper, awake! How long will you slumber?"—we are invited to understand this as translating the copenetration of human intellect and Holy Spirit. This teaches the desire for an other world, so that one can no longer be satisfied with the one of sense and imagination, while at the same time offering itself as a guide toward the higher realities.

Al-Burāq, the fabulous winged steed, appears a creature halfway between donkey and mule—this hybridity translates the ability of the Holy Spirit, intermediary between human and universal intelligence, to make the intellect active and to transport it across the spiritual realities for which it is made. Its human face (which in iconography is a woman's) is the sign of its role in instructing the human condition as to what it has to be.

Before the arrival at the holy House in Jerusalem, which represents the entrance to the world of spiritual realities, the story speaks of a woman who calls out to the Prophet—this is the faculty of imagination, surely, that beautifies the things of the sensible world for our eyes. Similarly, when, before the beginning the ascent properly speaking, he is offered the choice of a goblet of wine or a goblet of milk (Avicenna's version adds a goblet of water), this turns out to refer to the bifurcation between the path of the appetites, which pulls downward, and that of the rational soul, which alone is capable of receiving the intelligibles (the water, in the version with three paths, is the natural soul that maintains animal life). One can note here too that the Holy Spirit incarnated by Gabriel helps him in this choice, presented in symbolic form.

We will not note each of the symbolic equivalences presented in the Avicennian commentary. There are many of them, starting with the different prophets, who represent as many faculties and are also associated with the Intelligences commanding the different heavens traversed, from the moon and fixed stars up to the "sea" that figures the First Intelligence. When the ultimate meeting with God takes place, Avicenna argues that language is not adequate for the human to speak the praise of the necessary Being and the incomparable pleasure that accompanies immersion in union. "You alone," the Prophet declares to God, "can sing your own praise." To say that the moment when intelligence reaches its end is also the one when language reaches its limit is also to indicate the meaning of the faculty of imagination. In fact, to be a prophet is not only to realize oneself in the ascent toward God before finally plunging into the ineffable as a mystic. To be a prophet is to come back to oneself and to the others; it is to address fellow humans. A prophet must come back down from the mountaintop to speak to humanity, because he is a legislator and "it is not proper [for the legislator] to show that he has a truth hidden behind himself that he is keeping from the people; in fact he must fend off the insinuation of such a possibility."[5]

Divine speech is not made of sounds and letters, certainly; but it speaks the languages of the children of Adam. It was necessary, then, in order to return to those he was charged with instructing, that the Prophet put into words what is of an order different from language made up of sensible images. This is precisely what is done by the imagination, in other words the faculty of putting into images that of which we could not have a sensible intuition. The Prophet must "make . . . known the majesty of God and his grandeur by means of symbols and examples taken from those things that are majestic and grand. . . . That his discourse contains symbols and illusions poses no inconvenience to those who, by nature, are apt to devoting themselves to speculative research."[6]

Images translate the experience of the truth by their force of evocation. They speak equally to all, but according to the nature of each one's spirit: from those who stop at the letter of what they express to those who are able to climb up to their source and go toward the intelligibles they designate. Images are offered to these spirits so that, by means of them, they in turn can undertake the ascent. Avicenna's text ends by returning to his initial point, as he now provides a demonstration for it: the nature and necessity of rational interpretation for those whose spirit is so inclined, because "it is not for everyone that the things of divine wisdom are made simple."[7]

What about the others? For them, images are sufficient, fulfilling in some way the function of protecting intelligible content, since when a rationalist explains an intelligible reality only other rationalists ought to follow him, without troubling strangers whose spirit holds to the sensible. The story itself, as a story, has enough in it to satisfy literalists who want, for example, the journey of the ascent to have been performed bodily. Still, Avicenna says, one would have to wonder why a sensible body would be the means of travel toward a destination that is spiritual.

As we have said, the story is also an invitation to ascension. This means that the journey toward the realization of the prophetic nature, that is to say, union with the universal Intelligence, is a capacity or potentiality inscribed in humanity in general. The Prophet, in this sense, is the complete human (this is why the Qur'an calls him a perfect *example*), who instructs others in the path leading to their own perfection. The "rational explication" of the prophetic story, therefore, is *also* ultimately mysticism. To become one with oneself in order to become one with the divine: here is the goal, which is achieved when, from the fine point of reason and intelligence, there blossoms the prophetic nature that can receive illumination.

To finish, let us return to the initial question, of a becoming-Islamic of philosophy and of its meaning. The text studied here makes it possible to see, concretely, what this can mean: it is not simply the translation of Greek philosophers in order to comment on them; it is also reading an Islamic story like the prophetic ascent in the light of Aristotle's *De anima*, for example, as it was commented on and appropriated by al-Farabi. The result is drawing the lesson that the ascension in this story is (also) a journey across the human faculties toward the realization of human nature. Such a reading might appear, indeed, heretical to partisans of self-closure, for whom Islam is in itself its own philosophy and has nothing to do with "pagan thought." Far from seeing in Greek philosophy the opening of a possibility to better know oneself, they consider dialogue between the story of the *Mi'rāj* and the *Treatise on the Soul* to be a deviation from the path traced by the Tradition. So it was said that Avicenna, since he demonstrated the human capacity to ascend toward the intelligibles and the realization of our prophetic nature, had declared himself able to do without the Prophet and the Revelation.

Think back to al-Ma'mun's dream: if revelation, in Aristotle's mouth, came after *reason* in the matter of saying what truth is, this should be understood not as the expression of a hierarchy, an ontological priority of the second over the first, but as that of a logical priority. Revelation must address itself to humans, and therefore they must be gifted with the capacity to understand it. This is also why Islam places so much emphasis on the simple humanity of its prophet, totally human but still a totally completed human. The Avicennian reading of the ascent says nothing other than that when it establishes that philosophy—which in this sense is perennial and belongs to no particular culture, not Greek then and not Islamic—is, as the exploration of what humans are and have to be, a path to better understanding oneself. This meaning of openness has always been defended by the *falāsifa* and is today, as we will see again, all the stakes of the question of philosophizing in Islam.

4

AGAINST PHILOSOPHY?

Too much ratiocination leads to infidelity, declare those who'd thus give their closed-off posture the form of a proverb. This is directed, no doubt, against the *falāsifa*, engaged in rationalist explication. It could just as well be directed against speculative theologians; as we have seen, Ash'arite theology had been, first of all, a reaction against the excesses of a Mu'tazilism that could seem to have substituted reason for God. Since the theological "conversion" of its founder, the Ash'arite School's task had been to counter rationalism by weighing the balance back toward the side of quietism. From this school, as well, came the most radical denunciations of the philosophers' "errors," some of those declared to be quite simply heresies manifesting their authors' infidelity.

Such a denunciation came from the Ash'arite theologian Abū Hamīd al-Ghazālī (1058–1111), whose name was transformed in the West into "Algazel," and who is often simply called Ghazālī. But Ghazālī did not direct his attacks from outside, speaking from his position as a theologian and mystic: he wanted, rather, by working from inside philosophical argumentation, to show that it was doomed to self-destruction. His radical critique of Islamic Aristotelianism, *The Incoherence of the Philosophers*, had been preceded by an attentive and meticulous study of the philosophical thought of his era, or, as his title put it, *The Intentions of the Philosophers*. The scrupulous fidelity with which he reproduced philosophical doctrines in a "complete and clear treatise," as he said in his preface, showing "a perfect knowledge" of their theses, has led some to say that Ghazālī claimed the theses of Aristotelianism as his own, while he himself saw this honest exposition as the necessary prologue to the "refutation" that would come later. Here is the paradox of Ghazālī: the book of *Intentions*, when translated into Latin at the end of the twelfth century (it was published in Venice, in 1506, under the Latin title of *Logica et Philosophia Algazelis Arabis*), became a precious manual for the study of the philosophy that the *Incoherence*, for its part, had pilloried. Beyond this, as we will see, his works of mysticism remained profoundly philosophical: the discourse against the philosophers, in the end, comes itself from a philosopher, as would be argued a century later by the author who responded to *The Incoherence of the Philosophers* with a book titled *The Incoherence of the Incoherence*—Averroes.

Ghazālī was born in the middle of the eleventh century, near Tūs in Persian Khorasan. His education began in his native city and continued in Nishapur, then an important intellectual center. He studied theology there, but also philosophy and logic, with a renowned Ash'arite master, al-Juwayni, until his death in 1084. He was also initiated into the doctrine and practice of Sufism. Ghazālī lived in a particularly troubled period of Muslim history. Since the middle of the eighth century, the world of Islam was nominally under the reign of the caliphs of the Abbasid dynasty. But in reality, Andalusia and Egypt were officially beyond their control. Andalusia was governed by the Ummayads of Spain, while, starting in the tenth century, Egypt was led by the Fatimid dynasty (909–1171), created when a descendant of Ali and Fatima established an independent Shi'ite power. The Abbasid caliphs themselves had been forced to acknowledge the sultanate of the Suljuks, who captured Baghdad in

1055, reliving Sunni power from a century of Shi'ite tutelage by the Būyīds of Iran. It was under the Seljuk Sultan Mālik Shah (who reigned from 1072 to 1092), and thanks to the friendship and protection of his vizier, Nizām al-Mulk (1018–1092), that Ghazālī, after his studies at Nishapur, engaged himself in a career teaching theology and jurisprudence. This eminent intellectual position had, in the conditions of the time, an unavoidable and marked political signification as well.

Political tensions superimposed themselves on the doctrinal and sectarian divisions that marked the era, which Ghazālī said, in an autobiographical text titled *Deliverance from Error*,[1] illustrated a prediction announced by the prophet of Islam: "My community will divide into seventy-three groups, and only one of them will be saved." After citing this prophetic tradition, Ghazālī added: "What he foretold has indeed almost come true."[2]

There was, then, an urgency to defending and illustrating sound doctrine: it was a matter of salvation. And all the better if working for salvation turned out to also be working in favor of the politics of the vizier Nizām al-Mulk, who aimed to develop the Sunnism that was the foundation of his power through education. To advance this goal, the vizier had created numerous centers of teaching, named *nizāmiyya* after him, whose mission was to propagate Ash'ari theology and the jurisprudence of the Shafi'i School. Ghazālī's own master al-Juwāyni had taught at the *nizāmiyya* of Nishapur; and in 1091, at the age of thirty-three, he in turn was charged with leading the one in Baghdad, capital of the empire, a role he performed with the greatest success. But in 1092 his protector the vizier was assassinated by an Ismā'īlī Shi'ite. At least, this is what the most circulated version of the story claimed; there is also another version according to which a struggle for power between the sultan and his vizier led to the assassination. Regardless, the Sultan Mālik Shah died that same year. Ghazālī successfully pursued his teaching career until 1095, when, just as he enjoyed immense renown in Baghdad, he abruptly resigned to lead a nomadic life, moving between Syria, Palestine, and the Hijāz. In his own account, it was only in mysticism that he was able to appease his anguish, disenchantment, and thirst for certitude. It was as a Sufi that he returned to teaching, eleven years after leaving it, under pressure from the new vizier Fakhr al-Mulk, this time in Nishapur, where he had done his own studies. Five years later, in 1111, he returned from there to his native town of Tūs to give up his soul.

When he took up service in the *nizāmiyya* system a second time, the young teacher, confident in his knowledge and his right to receive the honors that accompanied his position, had given way to a different man, one who, coming out of an eleven-year retreat, accepted what he now saw as a sacred vocation. He wrote in his autobiography: "In myself I know that even if I went back to the work of disseminating knowledge, yet I did not go back. To go back is to return to the previous state of things. Previously, however, I had been disseminating the knowledge by which worldly success is attained; by word and deed I had called men to it; and that had been my intention. But now I am calling men to the knowledge whereby worldly success is given up and its low position in the scale of real worth is recognized. . . . It is my earnest longing that I may make myself and others better."[3]

What had happened? The profound crisis is which he found himself, which had finally rendered him incapable of teaching, had followed his posing himself the radical question of truth, which became for him an existential question: Can we attain certitude, where truth comes accompanied by its own proof? Are we condemned to skepticism? This crisis and its resolution are narrated in the "confessions" that make up the *Deliverance from Error*. Where to find certitude? Ghazālī recounts that he began to examine this question by considering the different answers that might be given by those who declared themselves partisans of the truth.

As would be expected, this champion of Sunni Islam rejects the possibility of encountering sure knowledge among the *ta'limites*, literally "those who follow the teaching of a master" (supposed to be infallible)—in other words, Shi'ites. As he presents it, this doctrine does nothing but defer the question by demanding it be posed to a master. As a theologian, but also as a philosopher, Ghazālī could speak against this attitude in the name of the personal judgment of those able to use reason. And as a theologian himself, he was familiar with the problem of the first group he considered, the doctors of Muslim scholasticism. Having charged themselves with the mission of defending an established and dogmatic tradition by the use of rational argumentation, the theologians either provided themselves a set of already-established premises or else became masters of eristic, destroying the reasoning of their adversaries: so there would be little hope of finding among them a method that seizes things by the root, establishing what is founded beyond any possibility of doubting.

Then there were the philosophers, who made just such a claim of radicality. Inept and uncertain when it comes to the quest for certitude, they are also, said Ghazālī, dangerous for truth itself. Are logic and mathematics, which make up part of the philosophical sciences, then dangerous? If they produce the impression that the truth of philosophy in general is of the same nature as the formal way in which their proofs demand adherence, then they run the risk, Ghazālī says, clearly speaking here as a theologian, of making religious truths pale in comparison. And those who, in reverse, speak against these, denouncing their insufficiency while claiming to speak in the name of religion, appear foolish and risk making what they so zealously place above the sciences appear simply as ignorance. Better, from the point of religion, to say nothing of them—this is the proper attitude.

But then there is physics and there is metaphysics, which have for their objects God and the things that He has created, of which philosophy claims to be able to speak truthfully, even if this truth is not a repetition of the one spoken by religion. Here lie, for Ghazālī, the errors and heresies of which the book *The Incoherence of the Philosophers* gives a systematic accounting. Twenty theses are held by the philosophers, Aristotle and his Muslim partisans Al-Farābī and Avicenna in particular, he declared. Seventeen of these would make the *falāsifa* worthy of excommunication for blameworthy innovation, while the other three are quite simply as many charges of heresy: first, the affirmation that bodies will not be resurrected and that punishment and recompense will be purely spiritual; second, the affirmation that God knows universals but that his knowledge does not concern particulars; and third and finally, the thesis of the eternity of the world against that of its creation ex nihilo. We will see later what explanation Averroes gave of these philosophical theses, along with his response to the accusation of heresy.

Let us return to the paradox of a condemnation of philosophers that is as radical as could be, excommunicating them, but that is itself a model of modern philosophy. "Modern" in the sense in which Descartes is said to be the "father" of modern philosophy, one that is written in the first person in order to proclaim the centrality of a subject that turns inward to encounter, within itself, the firm soil of certitude on which the edifice of knowledge can be raised. Ghazālī's procedure, which sets itself to doubt everything in its quest for certitude, has often been compared to the methodology of the author of the *Meditations*. Like Descartes later on, the Ash'ari theologian applied, to the sources of our knowledge, a principle of economy that says that if one of them deceives me at times, I must prudently assume that it always deceives me. First of all are the senses, whose evidence should be put in doubt in accordance with this principle: because I know, from experience, that at times they make me see things otherwise than how they are, I should behave as if they always make me fall into error. Then there is reason, with its logical and mathematical truths. Can I doubt that geometrical figures, those beings of reason that are free from the imperfections that attach to sensible things, have with certainty the properties that I can demonstrate? Can I doubt that ten is greater than three? Can I doubt the principle of noncontradiction, for example, which says that a thing cannot be itself and its contrary at once?

At this point in his method, famously, Descartes imagines that an evil genius dedicated to misleading me causes me to believe all these things that reason presents to me as absolutely true. An equivalent to this mechanism, minus the fantasy, can be found in

Ghazālī. For him, it is the senses that speak against reason by saying this to the doubting subject: scrupulously apply the lesson that you learned from us—knowing, through reason, that the moon is infinitely larger than it appears to you does not keep you from continuing to see it as the size of an orange; we make you see things under some aspect or another and without the faculty of reason you would have no way of knowing that they are, in reality, otherwise. So, how can you be certain that there is not a faculty X that could speak against reason in the same way that it speaks against us, some suprarational "eye" that would make you see the falseness of "ten is greater than three" in the same way that the eye of reason indicates to you that the stick in the water that the eye of your senses shows you as broken is in fact straight?

At this stage, perplexity develops. For Descartes, escape is through the door of reason; the condition for the evil genius making me think false things is that I think—so then let him deceive me as much as he will, declares confidently the modern man, master of himself and of nature. For Ghazālī, one leaves perplexity through mysticism. The truest state of perplexity is, in itself, a prayer, the most authentic that there is. All of being, in this state, takes measure of its total impotence, its absolute poverty, and its radical ignorance, and so entirely becomes an appeal toward power, wealth, and knowledge, the one sincere prayer to which God, as he has promised, is obliged to respond. This is why, for Ghazālī, perplexity, in its paroxysm, untangles itself from the inside as God projects the light of certitude into the heart. The faculty X whose possibility the senses indicated, this suprarational "eye" of which the senses gave the hypothesis, now fully becomes a reality.

Ghazālī's attack against philosophy, therefore, took two forms. The first is direct: the Ash'arite theologian judges that rationalism goes too far when it denies the resurrection of the body and that divine knowledge is concerned with particulars; this corresponds with al-Ash'ari's own reaction to what he considered to be the rationalist *hubris* of Mu'tazilism. Ghazālī pushes this attack toward intimidation when he speaks of heresy. The second form consists in referring reason back to its own insufficiency: it cannot be its own foundation. Given over to its own forces it leads to perplexity. We are therefore invited to turn our backs on philosophical ratiocination in order to better expose the "heart" (another name for the faculty X) to divine effusion. Among all the categories of those seeking out and pursuing the truth, Ghazālī concludes at the end of his journey, only the Sufis know the experience of certitude—that is to say, know a truth that comes carrying its own proof, a truth that is recognizable, unmistakably and immediately, by its *taste*.

One of the principal targets of Ghazālī's attack on philosophy is Avicenna. He attributes to him the thesis that the reality of prophecy is simply wisdom to the point that, ultimately, a friend of wisdom can do without the revealed prescriptions. To such a thesis Ghazālī opposes "faith in prophecy," which for him flows not only from the certitude that there exists a faculty beyond reason just as reason is beyond the senses, but also and above all from considering the personality of the Prophet and, in particular, his compassion for creatures, translating an experience located elsewhere than in the philosophy produced by our capacity of knowing. Doubtlessly, in saying this Ghazālī was thinking of the way in which the Qur'an exalts not the cognitive faculties of the Prophet but "the excellence of his character." But, then, does the difference between Avicenna and Ghazālī really lie in the nature of what they say about human faculties and prophetic knowledge?

Consider the text of Ghazālī titled *The Niche of Lights*, which is a mystical and philosophical commentary of a Quranic verse that compares God to light: "God is the light of the heavens and the earth. His light is like a niche in which is a lantern, the lantern in a glass, the glass like a shimmering star, kindled from a blessed tree, an olive, neither of the East nor the West, its oil almost aglow although untouched by fire. Light upon light!" (24:35).

In *The Niche of Lights*, Ghazālī speaks of the *Mi'rāj*, the ascension that leads from light to light up to the only true light, that of God. He begins by establishing a hierarchy between dark bodies and those that are illuminated, those that, like the lamp, the sun, or the flame, are in themselves sources of light. The eye that perceives luminous or illuminated objects, he then says, more than the bodies themselves, deserves to be called "light." If one then considers the imperfections of the sensible eye, which is subject to error, one admits the need, in order to find the light, to continue to rise up to the eye of reason, which must exercise a veritable reign over the five senses and also over the imagination, reflection, memory. This rational faculty opens onto a world said to be higher, spiritual, and luminous in relation to the one below, the shadowy world of the sensible. In the same way that this world is illuminated by the light of the sun, the other takes its light from a "lamp that illuminates" and that is the "holy prophetic spirit."

It is this faculty, Ghazalī says, to which the Quranic description of an oil "almost aglow although untouched by fire" applies, one that, when this occurs, becomes "light upon light." The world above, as is discovered through ascension, is itself a hierarchy of lights that are the successive reverberations of the one and only source, just as, Ghazālī says, the sun gives its light to the moon, which is in turn captured by a mirror that sends the reflection against a wall. Only this first Source exists, because to be is to be light; all that is gets its being from it and manifests it. There is no other reality than its reality, no other light than *the* light. It eternally is, and its manifestation is eternal as well.

This, then, is how Ghazālī explains not only the words of the mystics who identify their finite and perishable ego with the divine infinity (the people of the elite, said Ghazālī, understand that the profession of faith, "there is no god but God," means "there is no other he than He," or "He alone is"), but also the reelaboration, by the same philosophers that he had excommunicated for affirming this, of the Aristotelian thesis that the world is coeternal with its creator. Ascension attains its ultimate point when plurality vanishes, and thus with it the separation of the created from what causes it to be. Whoever knows this, Ghazālī says, knows it, and whoever denies it is simply ignorant. This statement is not a tautology but the explication of that certitude beyond which there is nothing more to search for (there is no faculty Y beyond X, in a chain that would then be endless): that one who obtains knowledge by taste, where the thing is as it is tasted, has nothing further to pursue, or how one cannot explain color to someone who cannot see or, as Ghazālī says with a certain pedagogical brutality in his *Letter to a Disciple*, sexual pleasure to the impotent.[4]

After this first chapter that lays out a cosmology of lights, Ghazālī dedicates the next to the "microcosm," that is to say, to the human and her various souls: the sensible, which receives sense data; the imaginal, which fixes in images that are retained in memory; the rational, which captures nonsensible meanings; the reflexive, which combines, evaluates, and draws conclusions; and finally the one said to be holy and prophetic since it is actualized and intense in prophets and saints who, through it, receive the lights of the world above. Ghazālī then says that the sensible soul is the "niche" of which the Light verse speaks; the imaginal is the glass, while the lamp figures the rational soul and the olive tree, whose oil gives a bright light with very little smoke, symbolizing reflection. Finally, the prophetic soul, which always burns with desire, is the oil "almost aglow though untouched by fire."

So then, Ghazālī as antiphilosopher, and particularly anti-Avicenna? We have seen him explain in what sense the eternity of the world can be understood, and explain the human soul and its faculties "through the allegory of the lamp," as Avicenna says when he gives this philosophical interpretation of the Quranic Light verse in his *Remarks and Admonitions*.[5] Ghazālī is, as Averroes would later remark, less distant from the philosophers and their theses than he admits. It is nonetheless true that the history of Islamic thought has remembered him essentially as the figure who, on the one hand, thundered against the Reason of the philosophers and declared it useless and dangerous in the field of "Islamic" knowledge, and who, on the other hand, reconciled theology and jurisprudence with Sufism, in turn stripped of its excesses and speaking a more sober language concerning the encounter of the human with the divine than the noisy identification with God that had led some Sufis to be condemned for heresy. At root, he appeared as having the constant concern, against the two elitisms of the philosophers and the mystics, of guarding the community in its entirety, keeping it in accord with doctrines and theses that contain nothing susceptible to destabilizing the way in which the great majority believes. This is why Sunni orthodoxy that speaks of him as *Imam* Ghazālī has also given him the title *hujjāt al-islām*, the "proof of Islam."

What, then, to make today of this major figure, a "proof of Islam" identified as the champion of one sect and theology to the exclusion of other interpretations who pronounced a verdict of excommunication against philosophical thought? "Proof of Islam" for the majority, Ghazālī is considered an impediment by those who, wishing to see Islam reconnect today with its principle of movement, judge that his historic role in the decline of philosophy in the Sunni world (the Shi'a world is another story) led in the direction of petrification. This is what, for example, the Indian modernist thinker Sayyid Ameer Ali (1849–1920) wrote in a highly influential book first published in 1891, *The Spirit of Islam*.[6] Citing another author who had gone so far as to say that "but for al-Ash'ari and al-Ghazālī the Arabs might have been a nation of Galileos, Keplers and Newtons," Ameer Ali meditates on the desire for conformity that leads to the repression of anything considered heresy, in particular rationalism and reformism, saying of Ghazālī that "this mystic Imam, by his quietism, froze the blood in the veins of the Muslim peoples and held back their energies from progress and development."[7]

Ghazālī, a historical figure of exclusion and quietism? He cannot be reduced to this, and he still speaks to us who, today, deem it vital for thought in Islam to advance critical spirit and pluralism. To this Ghazālī, no longer exclusionist but pluralist, we will return in this book's last chapter.

5

A LESSON IN ECOLOGICAL PHILOSOPHY

Did he come out of a woman's womb, or was he the fruit of spontaneous generation? This question opens a philosophical novel that was undoubtedly an inspiration for the author of *Robinson Crusoe*, and that also bears its hero's name as a title: *Hayy ibn Yaqzān*, literally "Living, Son of Aware." This novel's author was the philosopher Abū Bakr ibn Tufayl, whom the Latin scholastics would call Abubacer. He was born in the first decade of the twelfth century, likely around 1105, in the Andalusian city of Guadix. He died at roughly age eighty, in 1185, in Marrakesh, Morocco. As his biography is little known, we can only hypothesize that he probably studied in Seville and Cordova, important centers of teaching in the region of Andalusia that history has remembered, at the height of its flowering, when it was dedicated to reason and Sufism, as an incarnation of pluralism and tolerance.

The south of Spain had been Muslim land, known by the name of Andalusia, since the start of the eighth century, when Arab and Moorish occupation turned it into a dependency of the Umayyad caliphate of Damascus. When this caliphate ended bloodily in the middle of the eighth century, to be replaced by the Abbasids, an

Umayyad prince who escaped found refuge in Andalusia and declared himself an "emir" in Cordova. In 929, one of his descendants established a caliphate of Cordova that would last for a century. This was a century of great flowering, above all intellectual, which made Cordova, like the city of Baghdad it emulated, a major center of Muslim and Jewish philosophy. The fragmentation of Andalusia into small kingdoms after 1031, the year the caliphate of Cordova ended, worked in favor of the Spanish Reconquista, which would continue until the end of the Muslim presence in 1492. In response to the Christian offensives, two great Muslim counteroffensives in particular were able to retake Andalusia for a time: that of the Almoravid Berbers who founded Marrakesh in 1062 as they set out to reunify the territory and to push back the Reconquista; and, after the decline of the Almoravid dynasty, that of the Almohad Berbers who, beginning in the middle of the twelfth century, reestablished a Muslim Spain after defeating the king of Castille at Alarcos in 1195.

Ibn Tufayl's life unfolded between Almoravids and Almohads. After practicing medicine in Granada, he settled in Marrakesh around 1154, where he was the friend and personal physician of the Almohad sultan Abū Ya'qub Yūsuf. To this sovereign, who had the marks of a "philosopher-king" and protector and friend of scholars, he presented Averroes, then around thirty years old, to whom he would later turn over, at his death, his responsibilities as the sultan's personal physician. Of the numerous works, especially in medicine and philosophy, that we know Ibn Tufayl to have authored, all that remains is the philosophical novel *Hayy ibn Yaqzān*.

Ibn Tufayl's work puts itself explicitly under the patronage of Avicennian philosophy. First of all, because Hayy ibn Yaqzān, along with Salāman and Absal, two other characters who appear in the novel, was a creation of Avicenna. Avicenna gave the name Hayy ibn Yaqzān to an allegorical character representing, in human form, the Active Intelligence. Ibn Tufayl's preface also explicitly mentions this philosophical patronage when he remarks that his work allows for understanding that state in which knowledge gives itself, in all its "sweetness" (the taste that Ghazālī spoke of), beyond speculative reason and the faculty of deduction, to those whose "inmost being becomes a polished mirror facing towards the truth."[1]

Ibn Tufayl thought up a novel whose hero, Hayy ibn Yaqzān, growing up alone on a deserted island, would give the proof that a solitary man who had never known the society of those like him, and with only the resources of reason for support, could from these sources alone discover all that man has ever known and all that man has ever been, up to the most sublime peak of his humanity. Even in absolute solitude, at the limit of his reason he can meet God and find Him worthy of adoration, and also find religion, which teaches him the ways to adore. In this movement of lifting himself up to the presence of the hidden God who gives answers to the questions that brought him there, he discovers that his condition is such that he cannot truly become what he is except by making peace with the whole world and the skies as well, that is, the stars that he discovers are his brothers. This is the condition for him to cease being the divided being he had been, and to finally surrender to himself, in peace with who he is. It can be noted in passing: to surrender to oneself and so make peace with God, as with oneself, could be a way of translating "Islam."

So Hayy is born from the earth—or maybe not. This novel, which is in this respect very modern, playing with possibilities long before Diderot did in *Jacques le Fataliste*, tells us that Hayy was probably the son of a princess, the secret fruit of an unfortunate passion for a man whom her position and her father both forbade her from loving. So, like a new Moses, he was entrusted to the waters that carried him to this island where he would learn to be born to himself, to the humanity that he would reinvent, alone, completely.

But then, no! Instead, he might have been a son of the earth, directly and without intermediary. The combination of ferments and telluric forces with favorable temperature, a natural conjunction of favorable factors, brought him into existence by what the ancients called equivocal or spontaneous generation. In this case he would have come to life first, before the divine light, projecting itself on his substance, set in motion his becoming-person.

But, on reflection, are these two births really so different? Whether the womb that carried him was a woman's or the Earth's, the biochemistry is the same when it comes to producing *life*, and the same divine intervention is required as the only thing able to make it a *being*. This play with possibilities, with its indifference toward the truth of the origin, indicates that at root what is really important in the birth of the Living is the depositing by God into his soul of the capacity and freedom that bring the human into being. This deposit is reason. Must this latter then pull itself away from Earth and against it realize humanity, thus rendering human beings "as it were masters and possessors of nature"? In the philosophical tale *Hayy ibn Yaqzān*, different answers are given to this question, at different moments of his existence, by the novel's hero.

First of all, in order to live he needs to fit himself into nature, to adapt to it, to melt into it—in short, to imitate; he needs to imitate his mother, the doe who raised him through his early childhood and who, along with the milk she gave him to nurse, taught him love. The death of his nurse pushes him out of his first innocence and teaches him astonishment, incomprehension, sadness, and solitude. And it is the chaos of emotions that her demise plunges him into that leads him to pose his first metaphysical question: What had become of the principle that had animated his mother and whose absence now made her unable to answer his cries, and would soon require him to put her into the earth? This question is the Ariadne's thread leading him to his capacity for reasoning and to the corollary notions of humanity and divinity.

So then, he begins by imitating his mother and the other animals around him. Once he discovers his hand and notes that it distinguishes him from the others around him by giving him the power to extend himself through tools that multiply his natural forces and his defenses, he applies the technical possibilities this opens to him in order to better inhabit the Earth—that is to say, to be part of it, form one body with it, and not to behave with it as if he were an empire within an empire. Then his reason, becoming a *libido sciendi*, an insatiable appetite for knowledge, leads him to behave with violence toward his environment and toward the other beings among which he lives, carried out in the good conscience of someone persuaded the Earth is at his service, convinced that things are subdued to his desire and also that they are as inexhaustible, as renewable, as this desire itself. He wants to know what animates beings, what it was that made his mother living and then, by its leaving, dead. At first, he tries to discover this by dissecting corpses. Then, convinced of his inability to find the principle of life in the dead, he tries to surprise it in the last breath an animal exhales, by moving on to disorderly vivisections. He has not yet learned to, first of all, respect the principle he hopes to grasp, being wholly prey to the hubris that seized him when he discovered his difference. It is this same difference, which he becomes conscious of, that then leads him to search in himself, to finally place himself in front of the "deposit" placed in him, which had always animated him without his knowing. And so he discovers, in his heart, the mirror inside him that alone can contain God.

We will pass over the ways in which he sees the repetitions of this illumination to which, more than to the princess or the Earth that gave birth to him, he owes his origin. Nor will we dwell on the encounter at the farthest limit of reasoning where this solitary recovers the whole heritage of humanity, ontogeny thus summarizing phylogeny, in the ineffable experience of the encounter between reason and mysticism. Instead we will look at the way in which the predator in him is eliminated, that conquering technical *hubris* of the *master and possessor of nature*. Once he reads in himself, as well as on the horizon, the final raison d'être of the things and beings, he understands that he has imperious duties toward the world and toward his ultimate cause, which taken together could be called a religion. First of all, he tells himself that if the world has a cause beyond what he can imagine, then a duty of humanity toward everything that exists and all that permits and maintains life is incumbent upon him. He will not kill except from need, and will take nothing living for his subsistence without first assuring that this life will be reproduced. Replant, reforest, give back what one takes from nature the possibility of rebirth, in short, in today's terms, ensure that one's action favor a sustainable development—this is how Hayy learns to think, and it is one of the most important lessons that his itinerary can offer us today.

Then there is the question of how to adore the Being which he comes to understand as the ultimate reason of things, and toward which he has duties. The reflection by which the Living decides on the form that this religion of thanksgiving should take is both apt and beautiful. He asks, Could I be the only one to experience the taste of this knowledge that I am now drunk with, and whose object has nothing that resembles it? Then, as a good Aristotelian who reads the skies or the stars as eternally moving in a circular and uniform movement in obedience to the nature of their quintessence, he understands these to be his brothers, whose directing principle, as the Stoics would say, is the same as his, and who thus know the One who can only be discovered by means of this principle. From them he takes circumambulation as a means of contemplating God and giving thanks to the Ultimate Reason; so he invents the ritual of turning periodically around a fixed point, which then becomes, as a result of this very ritual, the center of the world.

This creation, by a solitary individual, of prayer in its cosmic significance echoes what Avicenna wrote in *Treatise on the Nature of Prayer*, where he notes that the "intention [of such a ritual] is to seek out resemblances with divine substances."[2] In circumambulation, the man that he has become recognizes the necessary Being at the same time that he harmonizes himself with the stars: now, born at first from earth, the Living has become the child of the stars.

The story of Hayy does not stop with this moment of the discovery of self, of God, of the world, and of the peace he makes with all beings so as to truly *inhabit* the earth, the duty of humanity that he has toward nature. The humanity that he met first of all in himself appears to him soon enough in the guise of another man, and then of an entire people, when one day Absal disembarks into his universe. The novel tells of Absal's arrival and his installation on this island to which he had decided to withdraw from the world, in order to live the life of an anchorite, which seemed to him more appropriate to his long-standing quest for the true meanings carried by the symbolism of his society's religion. Frustrated with his compatriots and their strictly literalist way of understanding religion, he found himself led to a meeting with another solitary, this one being alone from necessity.

Ibn Tufayl describes their meeting with plenty of novelistic detail, dwelling on the time it takes for someone who thought himself the child of a doe to recognize in the newly arrived another like himself. After having observed Absal while hiding, and noting the state of mind of this man who had come to make a retreat on "his" island, noticing Absal's tears, he can see in him "one of those beings who know the Truth"[3]—crying is a property of man. Once they finally meet, the friendship that quickly develops between them leads the two men to understand that positive, instituted religion, with its commandments and rituals, is nothing other than a formalization of the call to which Hayy responded, which spoke to him in the love of a doe and then in her death, in the warmth and light of fire, in the song of the stars, and finally in the effusions of life that his heart learned to receive, along the path where his intelligence had guided him.

Hayy had never needed to speak the language of humans. Absal teaches it to him at the same time that he presents the religion of his society, which he comes to fully understand, and which he reaches through contact with the pure faith of his new friend. *Through contact*—that is to say, from seeing himself mirrored in him, more than through explanation. On the contrary, it is he who has to explain to Hayy the laws and rituals that a prophet, long ago, established for humans as a translation of the commandment of God. What the Living then begins to understand, which will appear to him factually later on, when he goes with Absal to live among his people for a time, is the immense problem of the relationship between being and language, and of how the sensible words, by pointing toward intelligible truths, at once translate and betray them, protecting and conserving them but also putting them in danger.

They translate and they betray.[4] Hayy recognizes, in Absal's descriptions of the teachings of the founder of the religion, that what is being spoken of is the divine world he discovered himself. But why present it in this way? he wonders. Why use the language of allegory in place of "the naked truth"? Clearly, this is the question of someone who has never needed to speak, who has experienced the junction of self-intimacy and the light of truth without needing to formulate it. For the beings of language that we are, this truth is retained in the imagination through figures that our words express, not as it is when it is naked, but as they have the power to name it.

Words protect and preserve the truth. Ghazālī interpreted the glass in the Light verse as representing the imagination. The glass must be so clean, so transparent that one does not notice it but believes oneself to have reached the thing itself rather than its imaginal echo; but it also must protect the light from the wind. The word, like the image that it represents, protects the truth and preserves it by allowing it to be evoked. Nevertheless, this evocation, once again, cannot be carried out except in the mode of allegory, since the intelligible cannot show itself "naked" in the sensible: it needs a veil that reveals it but can hide it as well. Here is a danger that has a name, as Hayy will discover: literalism.

In the novel, Salāmān personifies this way of seeing, that is to say, an attachment to the letter and a refusal, Ibn Tufayl tells us, of "allegorical interpretation, free examination, and speculation." And it is Salāmān who is the ruler, with the capacity to put force at the service of established convictions. When Hayy tries to show the wisest among the people the verities beyond the exoteric sense to which they are attached, he realizes that the discipline of the arcane is necessary as long as humans differ from one another, dominated as they are by different "spirits." So it is in the name of this discipline

that the Living and his friend Absal return to their island to redis-
cover the truth of restlessness while leaving Salāmān's people to
their established truths, their rigidified fidelity, and a religion from
which life has departed.

6

THE OBLIGATION
TO PHILOSOPHIZE

Thus speaks the Qur'an: "It is He who sent down the Book upon you. In it are verses precise in meaning: these are the very heart of the Book. Others are ambiguous. Those in whose heart is waywardness pursue what is ambiguous therein, seeking discord and seeking to unravel its interpretation. But none knows its interpretation save God. And those deeply rooted in knowledge say: 'We believe in it. All is from our Lord'" (3:7).

Unless, that is, the sacred text has spoken otherwise, so that, in reality, the passage should be read this way: "*none knows its interpretation save God and those deeply rooted in knowledge. They say: 'We believe in it. All is from our Lord.'*"

Either God alone knows the interpretation of verses whose meaning does not appear clearly established, or else people "deeply rooted in knowledge" participate, as well, in this divine knowledge. These two readings, clearly, are not at all the same. How, then, can they both be possible?

It is important to know that in the first forms of its transcription, the Quranic text contained neither diacritical marks nor punctuation. These signs were added later, for obvious reasons of clarity; but it was not always possible to decide categorically where to cut off a phrase and with what punctuation mark. This is why, depending on the choices made, the passage on scholars "deeply rooted in knowledge" may refer either to witnesses of a knowledge belonging only to God, which one must have the wisdom not to try to penetrate, or, on the contrary, to partners in the knowledge of an interpretation that they alone are able to reach. What reasoning will allow a choice in favor of one meaning or the other?

First of all, it can be said that, when dealing with a sacred text, if at least two readings, depending on punctuation, are possible, this is not by chance: the Book itself meant to speak in both of the two senses. So then, from one side, it is possible to hold to a prudently quietist reading and say that if God enveloped some aspect or another of his speech with a certain protective mystery, this was to underline its transcendence beyond all that human intelligence can grasp. From another side, it is possible to begin from the principle that this word is expressed in "the language of the children of Adam"—and what sense would there be in inserting into a message addressed to them signs that absolutely no one is capable of deciphering, that tell them absolutely nothing? It then must be that these signs serve as tests, functioning to pick out those who are "deeply rooted in knowledge." Now those could only be the philosophers, someone who is a philosopher himself would declare, namely, the Andalusian Averroes, whose name today is the very symbol of rationalism in Islam.

Averroes was born Abū Walīd Muḥammad ibn Aḥmad ibn Rushd in Cordova in the year 1126. His family name, Ibn Rushd, which means "son of uprightness," would pass through different avatars— Aben Roshd, Aberrosh, Ibn Rosdin—before settling, in the Medieval West, as Averroes. He descended from a line of celebrated jurists in which his grandfather, whose name he also shared, was particularly distinguished; this destined him to a career as a high magistrate. He received the finest formation as a jurist, and equally so as a physician and a philosopher.

His meeting with the philosopher Ibn Tufayl had a decisive influence on the course of his career and intellectual life. Averroes himself told the story of how he was presented to the Almohad sultan Abū Ya'qub Yūsuf (who, at the time, was only governor of Seville) by his mentor, the author of *Hayy ibn Yaqzān*. Here is how a chronicler reported the story: "When I entered into the presence of the Prince of the Believers, Abū Ya'qūb, I found him alone with Abū Bakr ibn Ṭufayl. Abū Ya'qūb began praising me, mentioning my family and my ancestors, and graciously including in his description things beyond my real merits. The first thing the Prince of the Believers said to me after asking me my name, my father's name, and my lineage, was, 'What is their opinion about the heavens?' referring to the philosophers. 'Are they eternal or created?' Reticence and fear took hold of me, and I began to make up some excuse and to deny being occupied with the science of philosophy, inasmuch as I was unaware of what Ibn Ṭufayl had decided with him. The Prince of the Believers, however, perceived my fear and reticence and turned to Ibn Ṭufayl. He began to speak with him about the question which he had asked me, and he mentioned what Aristotle, Plato, and all the philosophers had said about it. Along with this, he presented the objections of the people of Islam regarding it. I thus saw in him a copious memory which I would not have expected even in one of those who are occupied with this matter full time. Thus he continued his exposition until eventually I spoke, and he came to know what I thought about that subject. For when I departed, he presented me with a monetary gift, a robe of high honor, and a mount."[1]

Reticence and fear at first, since he found himself being questioned on one of the themes on which theological orthodoxy had accused the philosophers of blindly following, into heresy in their opinion, the pagan Greek thinkers rather than the letter of Quranic creationism; relief and confidence later once he became aware that the "Prince of the Believers" belonged to the race of philosopher-kings, and that he was thus among kindred spirits. These two attitudes perfectly express Averroes's views on the responsibility of the people of interpretation, those who are "deeply rooted in knowl-edge": in one part, to hold their discussions at a distance from those who are of another spirit and, in the other, to declare the philosoph-ical truth of analogies and religious allegories.

Following the direction marked by Ibn Tufayl's arranging this first meeting between him and the Almohad sovereign, Aver-roes succeeded him in 1182, when Ibn Tufayl felt he had reached the age to pass on his role as the sultan's physician. According to the chronicler, it was also in response to a complaint by the "Prince of the Faithful" that there was too much obscurity in Aristotle's works and their translations that Ibn Tufayl encouraged Averroes to set out on his cycle of *Commentaries* on the Stagirite's different books. So he became known, in the history of philosophy, as "the Commentator."

Two years after Averroes's official entry into the sultan's closest circle, the latter died in 1184 during a battle that turned against the Portuguese armies at Santarem. His son, Abū Yūsuf Ya'qub, called al-Mansūr (the Victorious), succeeded him. Al-Mansūr was not a phi-losopher, but more of a theologian; and if he retained his father's doctor as his own and gave him an honorary position in his closest circles, the two did not at all share the same "spirit."

Numerous figures of the intellectual world, likewise not shar-ing this "spirit," accused Averroes before the sultan of having professed in his writings ideas contrary to the religious Law. The sov-ereign, in a political climate where he found it expedient to satisfy the adversaries of "those involved in philosophy," as an official decree described them, finally condemned him in 1197 to exile in Lucena, about a hundred kilometers from Cordova. The several months that this period of disgrace lasted gave his enemies the opportunity to celebrate his humiliation. In particular, certain writers of verses wrote very popular epigrams offering derisive treatments of those Renan would call the "philosophical party," and in particular Averroes, who had just been sacrificed to the "religious party." When the sultan's pardon finally arrived and brought his return to grace, the Commentator did not have long left to live. After revoking his own edicts against the philosopher, al-Mansūr called him back to his court in Marrakesh, where he died at the end of 1198. He was first buried there, in Moroccan earth, before his remains were transferred three months later to his native city of Cordova.

"None knows its interpretation save God and those deeply rooted in knowledge." In Averroes's interpretation, these are none other than the philosophers. But then what is the exorbitant privilege that merits their being admitted to God's secret? Could there be a more stubborn, and risky, response to the condemnation of the *falsafa* pronounced by Ghazālī, whose thought was held in high honor in the Andalusia of the Almohads? Averroes replied to the attack against philosophy in the name of religion by maintaining that in reality there is a harmony between the two, and he wrote a treatise, which he termed *decisive*, whose object is precisely to demonstrate this harmony.[2] The *Decisive Treatise on the Agreement of Religion and Philosophy* does not take a defensive posture: to the contrary, Averroes declares without hesitation that the study of philosophy is itself even a legal obligation.

As a jurist, by family tradition and by education, he began by recalling the major categories of Islamic law that divide human actions into those that are permitted, those that are forbidden, and those that are recommended. To these can be added those that are obligatory and those that are reprehensible. He then evoked numerous Qur'anic verses such as the following: "Or have they not contemplated the kingdom of the heavens and the earth and all the things God has created? Do they not see that their destiny has perhaps drawn near?" (7:185). Or this one: "Will they not consider how camels were created? How the sky was uplifted? How the mountains were moored? How the earth was smoothed?" (88:17–20). These verses share an insistence on the idea, which in fact recurs often in the Qur'an, that to reflect and meditate on what God has created leads to the knowledge of the author of all things. This knowledge belongs, of course, to the category of obligatory actions. Averroes could then put forward this irrefutable syllogism:

Meditating on what is leads to knowledge of the author of all
    things
The knowledge of the author of all things is an obligation
Consequently, meditating on what is is an obligation.

To this syllogism can be added a premise the Commentator advanced:
philosophy can be defined as meditation on what is. Here, then, is
Averroes's extraordinary assertion, the most assured of counterat-
tacks, that the study of philosophy, ultimately, is a religious duty. At
least, this holds for those who have the type of spiritual disposition
required. This restriction must be made, in fact, and is occasioned by
the differences that exist between individuals and their ways of
thinking.

Of what nature are these differences? Aristotle described a distinction between three types of arguments leading to conviction.
There are rhetorical arguments, which persuade by means of what
strikes the imagination and so gain the adherence of those whose
form of spirit predisposes them to be so convinced. Then there are
syllogisms whose conclusions impose their validity on whoever
admits their presuppositions; but these syllogisms remain dialectical in that their premises, even when they might impose on everyone, are still by nature only probable. In this they differ from the
assured premises that produce equally assured conclusions in
demonstrative syllogisms.

Ghazālī, we can recall, had used the same Aristotelian distinction in saying that the theologians' dialectical reasonings had not
been able to give him the taste of certainty he sought. To rhetorical, dialectical, and demonstrative arguments correspond the
"spirits" inclined to give them assent. Averroes asserts that the philosophers' demonstrative spirit is what makes them scholars "deeply
rooted in knowledge," those who can and must interpret divine
speech. It is their obligation to attain a demonstrative knowledge of
the Being and of beings, and therefore to first of all understand what
demonstration is, and to obtain a perfect mastery of that tool—the
Organon of philosophical sciences—that is Aristotelian logic.

And don't let the literalists, self-proclaimed guardians of an orthodoxy they have constructed themselves, complain that this amounts to sending Muslim scholars to the schools of non-Muslim masters! Averroes replies to them by saying that jurisprudence, the religious science par excellence and the discipline those guardians of orthodoxy hold to be the queen of the sciences, is itself nothing more than the art of producing juridical syllogisms, that is to say, of deducing from what is given in the sacred text and in the traditions accepted as precedent what legal consequence should be established. With the rationalist assurance that characterizes his thought he writes that if it is obligatory for jurists to obtain knowledge of juridical logic, how much stronger the obligation must be, on those who seek intellection of God and of his creation, to understand the nature of demonstrative reasoning.

But, once again, logic is no more than an instrument, and its study merely a propaedeutic to lead toward true, philosophical knowledge. Should its study be seen as dangerous, as Ghazālī said? No more than a remedy might be, if not administered as it should be. If there is a danger, this is by accident and not by nature. But above all—and this is the heart of Averroes's rationalist lesson—there is no need to protect the revelation from philosophical reason, since the truth cannot be in conflict with itself, and demonstrative truth cannot speak against that of Scripture. The Andalusian philosopher's claims, like, in fact, the dream dialogue between the caliph al-Ma'mun and Aristotle, can find a justification in the Islamic tradition that says that the first thing to be created was reason. Surely the capacity for understanding the truth must first be present so that, subsequently, that truth can be presented, in person, in revelation.

At any rate, Averroes admits, with those who are afraid of philosophy, that it is not good for the spirit of demonstration to speak in its language to the "masses." This would only trouble them, and introduce confusion and division into the very heart of their thinking. Woe to him through whom comes the offense of internal division! The reason for the discipline of the arcane is exactly to avoid seeing this occur. Averroes liked to recall a prescription of Ali, the fourth caliph of Islam: speak to the people in a language they can understand, so as to avoid making a liar of God and his messenger. The author of the *Decisive Treatise* develops this discipline of the arcane to the point that he calls for governments to exercise a certain censorship on the circulation of ideas and books! This would preserve, as Ghazālī wished, the consensus that holds together the community, and would assure that philosophical arguments do not fall into the hands of those who lack the spirit of demonstration.

But once again, what is this exorbitant privilege that those who claim to be rooted in knowledge accord themselves? Is the revealed Word effectively a philosophical treatise of which only they have the key and the full understanding? Is the God of Abraham, Isaac, and Jacob in reality the God of the philosophers? The response to these questions is that, when faced with the truth of revelation, demonstration has no privilege over the other ways in which the word of God gives itself to human understanding. The specificity and the inimitable character of the divine writing come from the way it speaks to each spirit in its own language, and thus can be all things to all people. It presents intelligible truths directly but also in images; it is demonstration while at the same time it is also dialectic and rhetoric.

How can one know when to interpret and when to take things according to the letter? This follows from the principle that truth does not contradict truth. If the revealed truth is clearly in accord with reason, no interpretation is necessary. But when there appears to be a contradiction between the two this is a sign that allegorical interpretation is needed, to bring together what is said and its true meaning.

Certainly, the case of obvious contradiction is a limit case. More numerous are ones where a given meaning in its literality poses no problem to reason, but nonetheless can be given an interpretation that, by placing it in a new light, designates an other, wholly different truth. Averroes returns to this question in the conclusion of another of his works dedicated to demonstrating the accord between religion and philosophy. This work is the *Exposition of Religious Arguments*, and its conclusion studies the "canon of interpretation." The question it raises, which comes before and leads to interpretation, is precisely that of knowing what should be interpreted and what should not be. The sign that indicates one should not interpret is not as simple to perceive as in the case of an obvious contradiction between text and reason; for this reason, the spirit of demonstration can only be acquired by philosophical *formation*, according to Averroes, if it is already in the individual's *nature*.

Because it is the role of those who are rooted in science to reconcile, by interpretation, what the text says and what reason demands even where no contradiction is apparent to those who do not have the same disposition, one can see, writes Averroes, why Ghazālī was able to claim that the philosophers spoke against what religion says regarding the creation of the world, God's knowledge of particulars, and the resurrection of the body. The root of the matter, for him, is simply that the theologian wanted to speak to all and in the name of all, without paying attention to the philosophers' right, with which he was quite familiar, to interpret, the right to take the text in a way that, without contradicting it, does not merely repeat it literally. If Averroes took the time to write *Incoherence of the Incoherence*, a point-by-point refutation of the attacks by which Ghazālī tried to prove "the incoherence of the philosophers," he also declared that, in the end, the Baghdad theologian's condemnations and excommunications should not be taken too seriously: he understood perfectly what the philosophers said, since he himself was one of them, even if he had assigned himself the mission of preserving the community from the confusion that the circulation of their interpretations could cause.

What, for example, is behind the discussion of God's knowledge of particular things? Nothing more, Averroes suggests, than the distinction between the way in which God knows and the way in which we understand knowledge as the effect produced in us by the thing known, including the alterations of which it has been the object.

God's eternal knowledge, which does not change, is to the contrary the *cause* of the object known. The latter, then, does not enter into divine knowledge; it flows from it.

Similarly, must one at all costs understand the creation of the world as the apparition, ex nihilo, of the creation, while up until then the creator had been without there being anything along with him? Is it not sufficient to consider the distinction between creator and created as that which exists between what is in itself and as its own cause and what draws its being from and is sustained in existence by other than itself? To say that the world is created is to say that it draws its existence from the God it manifests. Finally, what Ghazālī presents as the third great heresy of the philosophers is less the negation of the resurrection of the body than the affirmation that the joys and sufferings in the world beyond, as described in the Qur'an, are so many allegories of the spiritual rewards and punishments known to souls.

Will spirits equally rooted in science necessarily give the same interpretation of a text? Clearly no; and here, certainly, is found the crucial problem of interpretation. The right to interpretation is also an open door to pluralism. But pluralism itself is not an evil, says Averroes (and one could think here of a prophetic saying that makes divergences between scholars a blessing): the problem arises when plural interpretations become factions, when groups seize onto ideas and attempt to impose them as true and exclusive of all others. Is this not, one could ask, precisely what strict attachment solely to the letter helps prevent, namely, the multiplicity fatally introduced by interpretation? The response is that the most literal meaning is already an interpretation. There is never, at root, a zero degree of interpretation. In the infinite pursuit of a meaning that always remains a horizon, literal signification is only one among the plurality of interpretations.

In 1997, the Egyptian director Youssef Chahine made a film dedicated to the life of Averroes, titled *Destiny*. The film opens with powerful images of a man in the south of France being led to a pyre under the horrified watch of his wife and son. His crime? He had been declared a heretic for having translated Averroes's books from Arabic. His last words are for his son Joseph, to whom he entrusts his mother and also, surely, his work, since this son then attempts to cross Spain in order to find, in Cordova, *the Commentator* for whose sake his father has been condemned to burn with his criminal manuscripts. The film closes, too, with the image of a fire, presenting Averroes's departure for exile in Lucarno against a background of tall and raging flames devouring his books: the sultan al-Mansūr ordered this immolation of the philosopher's works in order to make overtures of good will to the "religious party."

Or rather, the fanatic party—since the filmmaker presents the Commentator's enemies, who use religion to attain power, with all the features of radicalized and manipulated extremists, adepts of terror with nothing but disdain for life. In retrospect, this very "Bollywood" film, with its Andalusian songs and dances, shows how Averroes, his close family, and his extended family of friends and disciples represent the power of knowledge, which is also the force and joy of living in love and tolerance. The immolation does not have the last word since, in the end, life triumphs over death when the philosopher learns that one of his disciples, the sultan's own son, has managed to carry copies of his work for safekeeping in Egypt. With bravura then, he tosses one of his books into the fire, over his shoulder and without looking back, while the screen displays, along with the words "The End," the moral of the story:

Thought has wings, no one can stop its flight.

Of course, philosophy did not disappear from the Muslim world with the Commentator's death. The Shi'a world, in particular, continued to explore the "Eastern wisdom" that Avicenna had tried to express at the end of his life. *The Book of Eastern Wisdom* was a title chosen by the philosopher Suhrawārdī,[3] who died in Aleppo in 1191, seven years before Averroes, another victim of intolerance: he was executed at the age of thirty-six, under obscure circumstances, by the order of Saladin and under the accusation of corrupting religion. *The Book of Eastern Wisdom* combines Platonism, elements of Zorastrianism, and Islam to construct an emanationist metaphysics of light: from God, Light of lights, proceeds a succession of lights, down to the souls that direct the heavens and the bodies of the sublunary world of generation and corruption. Returning to God is leaving Western exile and *orienting* oneself, that is to say, turning toward the "East" from which illumination comes.

Suhrawārdī's work would continue to nourish philosophical thought, in the Persian world above all. In the thirteenth century Qotboddīn Shīrazī produced a commentary that was in turn reflected in the seventeenth-century interpretation given by Mollā Sadrā, who, Christian Jambet tells us, founded a Shi'ite ontology.[4] In a general sense, the Persian theosophical universe would be characterized by a continuity of philosophical thought linked to imamology (that is to say, reflection on the cosmic significance of the succession of the imams), a continuity that no longer exists in the Sunni world. The death of Averroes, then, announced the end of an epoch and perhaps the triumph of those who attacked *falsafa* as a science foreign to the Islamic religion.

Chahine's message is ultimately this: it is urgent to once again give Islam the face of reason, that is to say, of pluralism, tolerance, and the never-satisfied quest for knowledge in every place where a "word of wisdom" can be found. *Destiny* presents the figure of Averroes as such a face, as a reminder of the need, today, to philosophize, following the example of the one who, better than anyone, expressed the spirit of Muslim Andalusia.

7

THE NEED FOR PHILOSOPHY

On March 29, 1883, Ernest Renan delivered a lecture at the Sorbonne titled "Islamism and Science," which was published the day after in the *Journal des Débats*. In it he treated the question of Islam as it was then posed, in terms enormously similar to ones we hear used today by those who think that they can read, in the events of our time, the signs of a cosmic conflict between irreconcilable cultures that has become our present and our horizon (a conflict they do not hesitate to call a "world" war, the third or fourth of that name depending on the status given to the "Cold War"). Renan begins from the postulate of the "actual inferiority . . . of the States governed by Islam," according to him the result of "the way in which the mind of a true believer is fatally limited, by the species of iron circle that surrounds his head, rendering it absolutely closed to knowledge, incapable of learning anything, or of being open to any new idea"; this condemns "the races that hold, from that religion alone, their culture and education" to a fanaticism that makes each of them "happy as with a privilege, with what makes his inferiority."[1]

He then evokes the opinion of those who see, based on the golden age of Muslim civilization, the promise of another, flourishing future on the horizon of Islam. That's incorrect, he declares: "Yes; from about the year 775 to nearly the middle of the thirteenth century, that is to say, for about five hundred years, there were in Mohammedan countries learned men, thinkers of very high distinction. It might almost be said that, during this period, the Mohammedan world was superior in intellectual culture to the Christian world";[2] but it should be known, Renan thunders, that this was not thanks to Islam, but *despite* the religion, and *against* it.

His demonstration rests on a thoroughly circular reasoning, which consists in identifying what he calls "Islamism" with Arabism, and then seeing all aspects of progress and openness as deriving from the non-Arab, thus not truly "Islamic," elements of the Muslim world. For Renan, an avowed racialist who believed in mental dispositions determined by ethnicity, the development this part of the world experienced was, at any rate, fundamentally Greek, carried first by the Nestorian Christians, then by the Iranian world (Aryan, of course); the Abbasid caliphs, like al-Ma'mun, who presided over cultural openings were "hardly Muslim," the two facts explaining each other, and the movement of thought open to "new ideas" was always in an inverse relation to the prominence of religion, which reached its peak when the caliphate became Ottoman and so fell to "the Turkish race" (non-Arab, one can't help but remark). At this moment, concluded Renan, Islam had "slain the science and philosophy within itself."[3]

A veritable hymn to science, which is reason itself, closed the French philosopher's "demonstration" that Islam is, in its essence, misology. After the publication of this lecture in the *Journal des débats*, Renan followed up in the issue from May 19, 1883, with what he would call, in the book *Discourses and Lectures*, an "Appendix to the preceding lecture." He introduced it thus: "A remarkably intelligent Afghan sheikh, visiting Paris, having published in the *Journal des Débats* of May 18th, 1883, some remarks upon the preceding lecture, I replied in the same journal the next day, as follows."[4] In the appendix we also learn that an encounter with this man in Paris had been at the origin of Renan's decision to present a public treatment on the subject of Islam and science. So who is this "Afghan sheikh" who gave the initial inspiration to Renan's lecture, and whose observations led him to write an appendix to his text?

This sheikh is Jamāl ad-Dīn Assadabādī, best known by the name "al-Afghānī," or simply "Afghani." In principle, his name indicates that Jamal al-Dīn was Afghan, born in Assadabād, a village close to the city of Kabul. Unless, that is, it refers to another village, also called Assadabād, this time located near Hamadān, in Iran. But if he is called Afghani, or in other words "the Afghan," there should be no doubt. Except that in other circumstances he gave his name not as "Afghanī" but as "Istanbulī," or as "Ṭussī" or "Rūmī." To ask after the identity of this Afghan sheikh Renan speaks of is to become lost in the different identities he spent his life inventing. Was he Afghan and Sunni, as he often declared? Or Persian and Sunni? Or Persian and Shi'ite? According to studies that have carefully examined sources and testimonies, it seems most likely that he was born in October or November 1838, and spent his earliest years in Iran, in a family of Shi'ite *sayyids* (that is to say, "nobles," descendants of the Prophet). Nikki Keddie, author of an often-referenced biography of Afghani,[5] says that he performed brilliant studies in the traditional disciplines of Islam, gaining a deep knowledge of Muslim philosophers as well as Sufis. The influence of Islamic philosophy, whose teaching was generalized in Iran, unlike in the Sunni world, can be particularly sensed in the reflections he wrote at the end of his life.

If he was Iranian and Shi'ite, why pass himself as a Sunni? One could refer to a tradition of dissimulation that Shi'a minorities had developed, for reasons of security, while living in the midst of a Sunni majority that had not always been tolerant toward them. And in his eventful life as a political agitator Afghani had often needed to dissimulate his identity, to the extent that with him one is never sure of having raised the final mask. Still, behind all the identities he took on he was constant in the mission he assigned himself, which made him into the father of reformism, particularly philosophical reformism, in Islam. He took this mission, as his texts show, from the situation in which he saw the Islamic world. Fallen, for the most part, under the yoke of countries like England, Holland, France, or Russia, the Muslim countries, in their state as dominated nations, had discovered the decadence into which they had fallen years ago. It was time, then, to heed these Qur'anic verses addressed to situations like the one they lived in: "God alters not what is in a people unless they alter what is in themselves"; and "God would never change a favor He bestowed upon a people unless they themselves had changed their inner selves" (13:11, 8:53).

Consequently, Afghani saw his task as contributing to the modification of what the Muslim world had become so as to reestablish the "blessing" it had known in the past, by realizing its unity, by permitting it to resist imperial forces, and above all by encouraging the forces of reason and modernity within it. A sine qua non condition for him to fulfill this mission was obviously that he be heard. And it was undoubtedly this, more than the political circumstance that led him to escape the repressive regime of the shah of Iran, that was the fundamental reason for his giving himself a Sunni identity: this made him part of the majority that had proclaimed itself faithful to the prophetic tradition, so that his voice of renewal could carry throughout the Muslim world. At root, being Sunni, Shi'ite, or something else was of little importance; the task that history demanded be fulfilled required transcending sectarianism and for his voice, from the start, to not be taken as coming from a particular location and so put out of play without even being heard. Afghani did not hide himself behind borrowed identities; each one of them was his own.

The mission he assigned himself dictated that he uproot himself, which he did during an eventful life spent traveling and attempting to influence the course of events. In 1857, he spent just over a year in India before performing the pilgrimage to Mecca. We find him again in Afghanistan, where he was a counselor to the king

Muhammad Azam Khan after his seizure of Kabul in 1866, a role in which he showed his opposition to Great Britain. When Shir Ali Khan seized Kabul in 1869 and became king, Afghani was forced to leave the country. He was in Egypt in the 1870s, where he spread his ideas in journals he often had a hand in founding, and where he found in Muhammad Abduh (1849–1905), one of the students in his courses on philosophy, a disciple who would himself become an important reformist.

Ever the agitator, he faced expulsion again in 1879. He then traveled widely: Istanbul, Saint Petersburg, Moscow, Munich, London, and Paris, where in 1884 he and Muhammad Abduh founded a journal in Arabic. Invited to Iran by the shah, he fell rapidly into disgrace, and was arrested and then banished from the country in 1891. He died in Istanbul, on March 9, 1897, and was buried there until 1944, when the Afghan government requested that his remains be returned to the country to which his name was attached; they were placed in a tomb that today is inside the University of Kabul.

So there we have the "Afghan sheikh" whose "objections" to Ernest Renan's lecture prompted a "response" that first of all praised him as a remarkably intelligent and enlightened man. Beyond Afghani himself, what Renan evoked and saluted was the existence of a "league of good spirits" whose members can be found anywhere in the world, in every culture. Because these individuals speak the language of reason, they also bear witness to the unity of the human spirit beyond the divisions and fanaticisms that religions create. What Renan saw, then, in this man who gave him the idea of a lecture on Islam and science was someone who had broken out of the enclosure of his religion to think freely in the manner of Avicenna or Averroes, whom he called "those great skeptics who for five centuries represented the tradition of the human spirit."[6] Of course, in keeping with the racialist obsession that was then in vogue, he did not fail to attribute the capacity of the "Afghan sheikh" for free thinking to the energy of his "Aryan spirit." Renan also gladly conceded to his interlocutor the one point, he said, on which he had disagreed: he had the impression that the criticism was directed solely at Islam. Referring to the case of Galileo, Renan clarified that it is revealed religion in general that is naturally hostile to science.

Afghani's objections, we can see, were far from the protest that one might have expected and that his disciples had hoped for. He gave Renan every reason to believe that his interlocutor and he were, essentially, in quasi-perfect agreement, being among "good spirits." In the conclusion of his "response," Afghani agrees with the author of *The Future of Science* that "so long as humanity exists, the struggle will not cease between dogma and free investigation, between religion and philosophy."[7] He is not concerned with affirming concordance by evoking a "harmony," real no matter how often misunderstood, between religion and philosophy posed as ways of saying the same thing, two different faces of the same truth. To the contrary, Afghani affirms the primary reality of struggle, of conflict, of what Kant had called an arena.

He agrees with Renan: to philosophize is not to establish on different, rational bases a truth already given in religion. That is theology's role. To philosophize is to take the risk of engaging oneself in the struggle that is free thought, not thought grown rigid around a will to a priori fidelity and doing nothing but close in on itself until it denies and finally negates itself. There is, Afghani added, a desperation in this combat, since on the one hand the masses do not love reason, and on the other there is no escaping the thirst, also a part of humanity, that science, however beautiful it may be, can never satisfy. This last, antipositivist point should be underlined: it reminds us that science in turn cannot close up on itself and take the place of philosophy, thus depleting human reason and the desire that constitutes it and is at work in it.

The masses do not love reason? Why not then keep to oneself, practicing a discipline of the arcane according to the tradition of the *falāsifa* and the Sufis, staying among fellow "good spirits"? All that Averroes had asked for was that the community in general be protected from philosophy, and the philosophers from the misology of the crowds. At times, Afghani seemed to speak in these terms, as can be observed in his epistolary exchange with Muhammad Abduh, where he gave this as the reason for his deciding not to translate into Arabic, so as to disseminate it in the Muslim world, his response to Renan. He sought to avoid wide diffusion of the way in which the "Sheikh" had acquiesced to the French philosopher's declaration that Islam suffocated science and philosophy in its breast.

That being said, Afghani was first of all a reformist, who could not tolerate separation between an elite, naturally cosmopolitan because it speaks the universal language of demonstration, and the masses who would then be constitutionally inclined to detest this language and to close up around a rigid fidelity of repetition. The reform called for by the situation of the Muslim world was above all a movement of the education of this world (*e-ducation*, we could write, insisting on the etymological meaning as an *exit from enclosure*), not a conversation between the enlightened. The struggle for thought cannot be separated from the struggle for a becoming-world of ideas.

The intellectual or scholar thus has a responsibility to educate, that is to say, to commit to the continuous reconstruction of fidelity in movement, against the petrification in which it is held by what we could call, to use the philosopher Gaston Berger's fortuitous expression, a *retrospective stubbornness*. This is why, even if he does note that the intellectual history of the Islamic world is in itself a counterargument to Renan's declarations, for Afghani the true response is situated in the decision to give oneself a different future, while understanding the real meaning of fidelity. What matters is not countering Renan by evoking the past, but deciding to stop giving him grounds for his arguments. It was in the name of the intellectual's responsibility to open up the future that the Afghan sheikh had already been directing attacks against the Muslim scholars of his time in the name of science and its requirements before he ever heard Renan's discourse.

On November 8, 1882, in fact, in a lecture titled "Discourse on 'Teaching' and 'Learning,'" that he gave at Albert Hall in Calcutta and which he addressed to "the Indian youth," he repeatedly pointed an accusatory finger at those whom he called "our scholars." Their duty, he said in substance, is to spread light in society, while here they had become so small-minded that, like weak candles, they could not even illuminate the room in which they found themselves. How could it be otherwise, since they had lost the sense of science as openness, an activity that belongs to no people or territory in particular, when they set out to make a division between a "European" and a "Muslim" science? How could it be otherwise when they had lost the spirit of the great questions that provoke and orient, if they no longer knew how to ask "Who are we?," "What is needed?," and "What ought we to do?" How could it be otherwise when they had lost the capacity for astonishment, astonishment that provokes searching, in the face of a world in transformation, where electricity, steamboats, and railways ruled? In a word, how could it be otherwise when they were not conscious of the need for philosophy in the situation where they found themselves, and their world with them?

It was indeed of philosophy and the enlightenment it spreads that Afghani spoke of in the hymn to science he pronounced during this lecture. Certainly, in its technological becoming science favors the progress of societies and explains the domination certain people have exercised over others over the course of history. And today the domination that Europe exercises over the Muslim world is, ultimately, that of science over ignorance. But modernity should not be confused with its signs and with the scientific and technological effects it produces. In its essence, it is first of all philosophical and is produced within the "mother-science" that is the "comprehensive soul" of the different sciences.[8]

The disciplines being studied were still Aristotelian, Afghani remarked, indicating where the rupture was situated: the "scholars" of the Muslim world still forbade themselves from thinking the world of Galileo, Newton, or Kepler. More than Galilean-Newtonian science properly speaking, what was needed was the vision of the world with which modern science is in solidarity, that of an open, "infinite" universe that replaces "the closed world" where they lived.[9] In this way, the reformer called the scholars of the Muslim world to what was, at base, a repetition, this time in regard to modern and contemporary philosophy, of the caliph al-Ma'mun's gesture toward Greek and Hellenistic thought.

But this involves not only poring over books, whether the work of Mollā Sadrā, traditionally studied in the Shi'ite world where he had been educated, or those of European modern philosophers. To the contrary, it involves performing the antischolastic movement of lifting one's eyes to the book of the world. Descartes had said that philosophy is a casting-open of doors and windows. In the same vein, Afghani declared that "a philosopher is someone whose mind is stimulated by all the events and parts of the world, not one who travels along a road like a blind man who does not know where its beginning and end are."[10]

8

THE PHILOSOPHY OF REFORM

Afghani contributed decisively to the development of a philosophy of reform, which has been and continues to be expressed in various ways. Renan saw reform as an exit from religion. Afghani considered it renewal and continuation, based on a true understanding of the spirit of religion. Breaking with a sclerotic scholasticism was the way to reconnect with the movement that religion initially is. If, as we have seen, the goal of reform was to bring on the advent of modernity, what content should we give to this term? Afghani's Egyptian disciple Muhammad Abduh gave what must be the clearest indication of what should be understood by modernity. In his *Theology of Unity*,[1] he explained that it is a matter of liberating reason from the chains of imitation—that is to say, from the blind and mechanical repetition of tradition—and affirming that the human is free and has attained its age of majority and that there is no master whose role exceeds the simple fact of awaking intelligence to itself and to its own capacities of judging.

It would be reasonable to say that the contents here given to modernity translate the influence of the thinkers of the Enlightenment, as they were developed in Europe; in fact, Abduh cites "a

Western philosopher" who says that the emancipation of the will and the autonomy of judgment are the foundations on which modern European world was built; but he adds that this foundation itself is the effect of a ray of light that came from Islamic culture and illuminated the sixteenth century in the West. Of course, this last proposition is primarily that of an apologist, but beyond its exaltation of the supposed influence of the Muslim religion its affirmation of an Islamicity of modernity *in the singular* presents three important aspects.

First of all, Abduh does not engage in a face-to-face confrontation with the West, trying to oppose to European modernity an alternative Islamic modernity. It is clear that he thought that modernity might, here or there, in this or that region of civilization, take on a particular color; but there is no less *a* modernity, because the core is everywhere the centrality of the rational subject, autonomous in its judgment.

Next, to say, as he does, that this modernity is the daughter of Islam is, in the final analysis, no more than a way of recognizing in all cultures a universal demand for emancipation through the promotion of the autonomous subject. The same thing is produced whenever the universal character of human rights is *recognized* by means of an appropriation that, for each different culture, consists in *recognizing itself* in the declaration of these rights.

The third aspect of Abduh's affirmation is what could be called the retrospective reconstruction of the meaning of religion. One can see this here: it is because today the autonomy of individual judgment appears as a value and a requirement that it is projected as a meaning that religion *has always* carried. This approach, revisiting the foundations to make them carriers of progressive demands posed by the present, is characteristic of reformist philosophy. It could be characterized as a progressive fundamentalism, as opposed to reactive fundamentalism.

The evocation of origins can translate into becoming clenched up around the desire to reproduce at all costs what was *in those times,* those of the golden age, the first generation. This attitude goes back to the belief that fidelity means the servile imitation of a model. This is, quite simply, impossible, since the model that is given is itself always reconstituted, that is to say, fabricated. Wanting to try to live like "the golden generation" is the same thing as affirming that there is an initial meaning, clear and evident in itself, in relation to which all others are nothing but interpretations.

Of how those who were there at the origin lived and thought, we know only a little. To want to do like them is inevitably to invent. To claim to reproduce the model of their actions without any innovation is to lie to oneself—because life itself, first of all, is innovation. This is why there is also a return to the foundations that signifies a search for inspiration in what was there at the origin, to try to capture the spirit of the religion, found in its initial free, revolutionary flowering, in order to better respond to the demands of the present and orient toward the future. Here what defines the "fundamental" is its distinction from the accessory, from the petrified interpretations that have interposed themselves between it and the demands of the present. One tries to restore the spirit of this fundamental and to reopen its future. This is progressive fundamentalism.

As for reactive, clenched-up fundamentalism, it expresses a horror of time, which it understands as what separates us from the original, more than from the fundamental. It is a reaction, just this side of violence, against the work of time, in which it sees nothing but the loss of what had been "in those times," those of the pious ancestors. Reactive fundamentalism howls desperately against time.

In many passages, the Qur'an speaks of people who oppose the preaching of the prophets in the name of their own faithfulness to the ways of their "fathers." Muhammad Abduh cites verse 43:21, which describes the rigidity of those who idolize the ancestors: "We found our forefathers set on this course, and are guided in their footsteps." He comments on it, declaring, essentially, the contemporaneity of this attitude. In effect, those who do not know that the project of liberating the human and its reason from the chains of imitation is a continuous movement can easily forget that this word of refusal is not only one put forward in a distant historical moment, when the word of God had not yet found a path into hearts and minds obstructed by idolatry: it is atemporal, in the sense that it is still ours, today, as we are called anew to the movement of leaving our enclosure in the tradition of the fathers, in petrified interpretations.

Modernity is nothing else but the understanding that life is the movement of always being in the process of coming out of tradition, of reason leaving its age of minority. In addition, understanding of this movement must itself be encouraged by meditation on past history. So, far from being simply what distances us from the golden age, time as history is a teacher of the truth that leads toward the future.

One finds the gesture of returning to the past to read a spirit of movement there and so to open up the future in the very title of a major book by Ameer Ali, an Indian modernist philosopher a dozen years younger than Afghani: *The Spirit of Islam: A History of the Evolution and Ideals of Islam, with a Life of the Prophet.* This book, first published in 1890, was reissued in a revised form in 1902 and again in 1922 with new revisions; in this final form it has been reissued many times up to the present.

Sayyid Ameer Ali was born in 1849 in Cuttack, the cultural capital of Orissa (now Odisha), in India, to a family who, as indicated by the title *sayyid*, traced its origins to the prophet Muhammad. He became one of the most eminent symbols of his time of the success that the British educational system promised to its Indian subjects, but that it had trouble convincing them of, particularly the Muslims who massively rejected English schools. After brilliant studies at the University of Calcutta, where he specialized in history, he began his training in jurisprudence in England in 1869, completing his studies in 1873. Following a career as a lawyer, he became a judge in the High Court of Calcutta in 1890. His life took place under the double sign of a Muslim nationalism confronting what he saw as the domination of the Hindu majority in India and a drive toward modernizing Islam through the development of modern education and a rationalist spirit.

This drive is at the origins of his reading of "the history of the evolution of the ideals of Islam" to uncover the "spirit" of this religion. In particular, his reflections on the status of women in Islam exemplifies the approach of a philosophy of reform that revisits the history of the foundations to discover in it an *intention* of the religion, to be pursued in the future.

But how then to be sure, when making use of this idea, which can seem totally subjective, that one is not simply arbitrarily projecting contrived readings and interpretations of the past onto our present questions? The *intention* must correspond to an objective movement clearly indicating a direction that can now be extended.

From this point of view, it is undeniable that the directives the Qur'an gives concerning the status of women move in a direction leading from the absence of rights in which they lived under a tribal law that was masculine in its essence to their recognition as legal subjects. Today one can deplore as inequality that a man's inheritance is twice that of a woman's. To think through this state of affairs and what ought to be done in the name of equality means first of all to be aware that this law put an end to the world of the tribe, where women not only had no part in inheritance but were themselves part of the goods to be inherited, their own will counting, naturally, for nothing.

In the same way, polygamy is associated with the Muslim religion today to such an extent that it often seems as if it was authorized by Islam as a new possibility offered to men of multiplying their number of wives. The fundamentalist reactions today to family codes in many Muslim countries that aim to accelerate the disappearance of this practice are themselves a reversal of things, behaving as if what is evidently only *tolerated* has become a condition sine qua non for the conformity of law and religion. This forgets that, to the contrary, the religious directives on this matter came to limit and codify the practice of polygamy, which until then had no rule apart from the will and desires of men. A maximum of four wives was thus set with the explicit condition that the husband must be just, and love and treat them with perfect equality. In this case, what does it mean that a verse of the Qur'an states that "you will not be able to act equitably with your women, even if you apply yourself to do so" (4:129)?

This, precisely, is what tells Ameer Ali that, in the end, the posing of the requirement of justice at the same time as stating its impossibility amounts to a pure and simple prohibition of polygamy.[2] The logical principle of contradiction and the clear indication that Quranic *directives* also provide a *direction* to be continued both lead, Ali explains, to such a conclusion. Beyond this, he adds, certain Mu'tazilite theologians since the third century of the Muslim era have drawn this conclusion from these premises. The Mu'tazilite, Ameer Ali declares, is by conviction a strict monogamist.[3]

This same approach, consisting in reading history for an indication of a future that responds to the urgent needs of the present, characterizes a work whose importance for the development of political philosophy in Islam cannot be too strongly underlined. Its title is *Islam and the Foundations of Political Power*, and its author the Egyptian Ali Abdel Razek (1888–1966).

After the declaration of the Republic of Turkey on October 29, 1923, the Ottoman caliphate, which had at least nominally remained the symbol of the unity and permanence of a Muslim community, was definitively abolished in March 1924, after first having been reduced to a purely spiritual function. With this officially ended the story of an Islamic world remaining just as it had been created by the prophetic message, even though in reality the idea of a central government that effectively administrated the affairs of Muslims, and that all of them saw as representing them, had been for a long time, perhaps even since the assassination of the third caliph, nothing but a fiction. As Islamic societies had been in fact directed by diverse local powers, the end of the caliphate changed nothing, in the final analysis, in the course of affairs. It nonetheless marked the end of a world, creating the obligation to rethink the political question of governance.

Was this a question of rethinking it, or rather of truly *thinking* it for the first time? Everything had taken place up until then, ultimately, as if the question of the political had been obscured, hidden behind that of the caliphate and the nomination of the caliph. Consequently, Abdel-Razek wrote in *Islam and the Foundations of Political Power*, a political science posing the question of the nature, particularities, and typology of government had never been developed.[4] In his book, published in 1925, the year following the abolition of the caliphate, he noted that philosophical thought, even in its initial vigor, had never seriously approached these questions by starting out from Plato's *Republic* or Aristotle's *Politics*, even though these philosophers' works were held in the highest respect.[5] There was a clear reason, itself political, for this absence, according to Abdel Razek: those enthroned do not want their power to be confronted with the question of its foundations, since this would risk laying bare the truth that they ultimately rest on repressive force alone, that they do not draw legitimacy from what they claim is a continuation of the prophetic mission. It is the very notion of continuation that must be interrogated, says Abdel Razek, since after all—and this is the provocative question that rattles through his work—was the Prophet a king?

Who was Ali Abdel Razek? He was, like Muhammad Abduh before him, above all a product of the venerable institution of al-Azhar in Cairo, the university created by the Fatimids, where, for centuries, many of the Muslim literati came to receive their training. Born in 1888 to a family of notables in Middle Egypt, with a reformist father who was a close friend of Muhammad Abduh, Ali Abdel Razek followed the *cursus honorum* of this prestigious university and obtained the title of *sheikh al-Azhar*, placing him among the most eminent jurists and theologians of the Muslim intellectual world.

What provoked the reflection that resulted in his work *The Foundations of Political Power* was the debate sparked by the publication of a work commissioned by the Turkish National Assembly in the form of a manifesto justifying the reduction of the caliphate to a spiritual significance and inviting Muslim peoples to freely define the forms of government appropriate to their situations. Many scholars had replied to this manifesto by insisting on the existence of an

Islamic model of the organization of power, resting on an "implicit Constitution," both of these deriving from the Prophet himself and commanding Muslims to an eternal search to conform to it.

Abdel Razek's approach, which returned to texts and tradition in order to demonstrate (*more geometrico*, as his translator and modern commentator Abdou Filali-Ansary explains in his introduction to the work) that there had never been anything like an ideal government that imposed an atemporal norm on the efforts of Muslim populations to find institutions that would represent them and administer their affairs, earned him a sort of trial carried out by the Council of Doctors of al-Azhar. At the end of this "trial," with its accusations and replies from the author—all of which gave a particular resonance to the "Ali Abdel Razek affair," as Filali-Ansary calls it—he was condemned to be excluded from the corps of doctors of al-Azhar, stripped of his title, and thus barred from teaching and being a judge. Apart from a few short publications, he would remain silent from then on, even when these measures were later reversed. He died in 1966, forty years after he published the work that has, to the present day, contributed most to the evolution of political philosophy in Islam by posing in radical terms the question of what fidelity was owed to the untraceable model of a government that would be at once, and indissolubly, both state and religion.

Observing facts as they have unfolded, and using reason to draw necessary consequences: here, said the sheikh of al-Azhar, is the method that should be used, and at the end of which we must confront the initial fact that the Prophet's religious preaching never had as its goal the constitution of a political state. Certainly, it had been necessary that he lead the radically new community that his message had instituted. But one can see that he was not preoccupied with laying out the principles of a system of governance and the rules on which it rested. If we know nothing, for example, of procedures for the perpetuation of the system, this is not due to a lack of historical information: it is because matters on that issue were left open and left to reason and human judgment.

What Abdel Razek reads in revisiting the history of origins is not a desire to see a new community achieve self-closure by erecting a model of indissoluble unity between state and religion, but an *intention* to inaugurate an open society where nothing forbids the thinking and construction of systems of government most appropriate to the conditions that the movement of life constantly gives birth to. Once again, the pressure of modernity is what leads to this retrospective reading, and the secularism on which modern Turkey chose to construct itself gave a good indication of how heavily this pressure weighed. But here is precisely the whole meaning of the philosophy of reform as illustrated by the method used by the book *The Foundations of Political Power*: to show that nothing in the *fundamentals* of religion is opposed to what modernity demands as the separation of state and religion, or to the development of a science of politics that has now claimed its own autonomy. To the contrary.

9

THE PHILOSOPHY OF MOVEMENT

That Islamic thought today is confronted with the challenge of changing times is evident. Confronting this challenge demands that we not adopt the image of a small boat facing turbulent waters. It is not good enough to merely state: "These are modern times"; we must *adapt*—from the outside, one could say—an already-constituted, solidified tradition to the changes that are arriving. Thinking in this way will only bring two formulas, equally devoid of meaning upon reflection, back to back: "modernize Islam" and "Islamicize modernity" are two opposed answers to the same poorly posed question. In fact, it is the point of departure for these two formulas that must be put into question; the false problem lies in setting our sights on modern times and Islam. Becoming must be understood otherwise, by realizing that time is not exterior to religion but is its texture. Time is not—or not only, or not first of all—a trial that religion must overcome, but constitutes its own self-deployment: time is God. Put differently, the response to the challenge of changing times, so as to continue the *intention* and emancipatory dynamic of the religion according to the demands of today, in the domains of social justice, of the equality of men and women, of respect for the principle of pluralism—in short, the necessary "reconstruction of religious thought in Islam"—requires bringing to light a thinking of time as creative becoming, a cosmology that would be continuous emergence, *élan vital*.

For a philosophy of *élan vital* to be possible, it was necessary to break with the direction imprinted on philosophical tradition following the paradoxes of the Eleatic thinkers: that of "Achilles frozen in mid-step" and of "the arrow that quivers, flies, and does not fly," as Paul Valéry described them.[1] That is to say, it was necessary to turn away from a conception of time as serial and divisible into instants. When the time of a race is understood only as the distance that separates the point of arrival from the point of departure and thus, as Aristotle defined it, the number of movement in respect of before and after, it is not time itself that is being thought but its transformation into space. If the movement of the race is thus spatialized as a collection of extremely tightly spaced immobilities, then its purely cinematic time easily leads to paradox. Achilles then would be the victim of a freeze-frame, while the tortoise goes quietly across the finish line.

Thinking time otherwise—or, rather, truly thinking it—begins with what the Senegalese philosopher Léopold Sédar Senghor called "the revolution of 1889," referring to the event that was the publication in that year of the *Essay on the Immediate Data of Consciousness* by Henri Bergson.[2] These well-known lines from the beginning of Bergson's work *Creative Evolution* present the truth of movement, beginning from the inside of a mental state, as not divisible into immobilities: "My mental state, as it advances on the road of time, is continually swelling with the duration which it accumulates: it goes on increasing—rolling upon itself, as a snowball on the snow."[3]

One day, when he was quite sick and forbidden to receive visitors, Bergson learned that an Indian, passing through Paris, had asked to see him. He made an exception and received him for two hours, during which they discussed, among other philosophical subjects, Berkeley's thought. This Indian guest, in a letter, reported on this visit and his conversation with the French philosopher with whom he had immediately sensed a profound spiritual affinity, and who, thanks to his having thought time as duration, had accompanied him along his path to *Reconstruct the Religious Thought in Islam*, the title of his major prose work.[4]

The caliph al-Ma'mun dreamed of Aristotle and understood that Islamic thought would develop in dialogue with the Stagirite and with Greek philosophy. It was in dialogue with Bergson above all, a French philosopher who was attracted to Catholicism but who remained to his last breath a son of Israel, that the philosophical work that remains the most important to a world of Islam seeking to reconnect with its own principle of movement would be founded: that of Bergson's Indian guest, Muhammad Iqbal.

Muhammad Iqbal was born on November 9, 1877, in Sialkot, in the Punjab region, to a family originally from Kashmir. His father was one of the Indian Muslims who were convinced of the benefits to be drawn, for Islam itself, from the modern education offered by British schooling. To their education in the tradition of Sufi Islam his older brother and he would add brilliant studies, as an engineer for the elder, and as a philosopher and jurist for the younger. In fact, after studying at Murray College (which would later be given his name) in his native city, and teaching philosophy for several years at Government College in Lahore, Iqbal went to Great Britain in 1905 to pursue doctoral studies in philosophy at Cambridge, at the same time obtaining a lawyer's diploma. In 1907 he completed a thesis in philosophy, *Metaphysics in Persia: Contribution to the History of Muslim Philosophy*. This would be published the next year in London.[5]

Iqbal had already been, for several years, a poet who was a pioneer in the development of modern Urdu literature. In poems he wrote before his European stay he expressed an Indian nationalism, as well as traditional Sufi themes. He then decided to write in what he called "the language of Islamic culture," that is to say, Farsi, in order to be able to speak more broadly to the Islamic world. In this language he published important philosophical poems: *Secrets of the Self* (1915), *The Mysteries of the Non-I* (1918), *The Message of the East* (1922), *The Book of Eternity* (1932). A series of lectures he gave in South

Indian universities in 1928 and 1929 was collected in 1930 under the title *Lectures on the Reconstruction of Religious Thought in Islam*. This book, which gathers together his thinking, illuminates his poetry, which in turn illustrates his philosophy.

Today Muhammad Iqbal's memory is venerated in Pakistan as that of a "father of the nation" and a monument of poetry whose verses are still sung. In the history, full of sound and fury, of Indian nationalists' attacks against the British colonial system, as well as the violent and repeated conflicts between the two components of this nationalism, Hindu and Muslim, Muhammad Iqbal played an important role from his election to the Punjab Legislative Council in 1926 until his death in 1938, including the decisive moment in 1930 when he was named president of the annual meeting of the Muslim League. In this role he spoke to the party of the perspective of the overwhelmingly Muslim-majority provinces of Punjab, North-West India, Sind, and Baluchistan forming "one single autonomous State within the British empire or without." Although he died nine years before the separate independences of India, Pakistan, and what would become Bangladesh, he has nonetheless been considered the father of the idea of a state for Indian Muslims existing alongside an India whose great majority is Hindu.

Despite this, the many rigidities today—political, religious, military—in the Pakistan he contributed to bringing into being constitute, as Charles Taylor writes, "a continual refutation of the very essence of his thought."[6] This thought is in fact directed precisely against "rigidities," the petrification of a reality whose nature is movement. If one word was needed to condense the whole of Iqbal's philosophy, that world could very well be *incompleteness*: incompleteness of the world, always in the process of happening; incompleteness of the human, always engaged in the task of accomplishing itself as a *person*.

Leibniz said of the monad's actions that they are the unfolding, in time, of what is in it *ab initio*, just as the logical subject envelops the totality of its predicates (*praedicatum inest subjecto*). At the same time, he insisted that, from the monad's point of view, its will is free in every action it carries out. Thus, to take one of the philosopher's favorite examples, Caesar has the free choice of crossing the Rubicon: the world is open to his action and his gesture will make History, that is to say, it will engage it in one direction or another. But from the point of view of the totality, that is to say, of the world that God in his wisdom has chosen to make exist, the decision of crossing the Rubicon is absolutely necessary. It has already been written, and the ink has already dried. In explaining that these two points of view are true together, that the world is open to the subject's freedom but also, since it is the best possible, necessary, Leibniz denies that he is justifying fatalism. Such a belief, he says, corresponds rather to the worldview or cosmology of Islam, and so he calls it *fatum mahometanum* or *fatum à la turque*. When Muhammad Iqbal established that the Quranic cosmology is that of a continuously emerging and open world, he also opposed the preconception that from the teaching of the Muslims' Book there arise, naturally, a belief that everything is already written and a closing-up of what Amartya Sen has called "the illusion of destiny."

For destiny can be understood in two different ways, manifested by the two attitudes they lead to. The first, which is what the concept of *fatum à la turque* aims at, is passive resignation before what is taken to be the will of God, all powerful and always coming from *outside*. To this attitude, says Iqbal, is opposed an active fatalism, of which the first is a perversion. In a word, active fatalism consists in believing, as is said, in *one's own* destiny, in believing that one's action coincides with that of the pen that writes what must be, since one is oneself the pen and the ink that trace this destiny. This is the fatalism of men and women of action.

As for passive fatalism, it is the consequence of total self-dispossession that stems from a conception of time and a cosmology that pose a closed universe in which the future, predetermined, is simply held in store, ready to be parceled out according to a fixed and inevitable schedule of events. This order can be considered, consequently, as constraining even the creative activity of God. This, says Iqbal, is a cosmology for astrologers, since for them alone does the idea of foresight have a sense: they *see* time as a given *space*.

As Bergson had said, we present what we think to be time to ourselves only by means of spatial images, of a river flowing or a geometrical line being drawn. We seem to have no choice but to use these images of time, since this is how the intellect that we have functions. To understand its object, this intellect begins by breaking it down into parts, and offers us only a serial, cinematic vision of time. This time, Iqbal says with Bergson, which appears as a series of moments each excluding the others, is a time that does nothing, deprived as it is of its living character. And it is linked to a universe that is itself a collection of finite things at the heart of a void where nothing happens.

To think differently, for the Indian poet and philosopher, means to reread the Quranic text knowing how to find the meaning behind the conventional image in which the idea of creation is enclosed: a completed action through which God would have produced the world with one stroke of his *fiat* to then contemplate its finished form. It means fully grasping the meaning of a prophetic tradition that Iqbal often cites, since it contains what is, in fact, the essence of his thought: "Do not vilify time, for time is God." What this tradition says is that time is not merely the site of being, but being itself, that to reduce it to space, so failing to truly think it, is also to fail to think being in its essential tension.

God is always at work in his creative act that is never exhausted, and the world that continuously springs out of this act is a world in movement. The universe, Iqbal thus writes, is not "a block universe," a finished product, immobile and incapable of change. He then adds this phrase that seems, in this prose text, to have been dictated by his poetic temperament: "Deep in its inner being lies, perhaps, the dream of a new birth."[7] Especially in his poetry, the highest expression of his philosophy, Iqbal sings the sublunar time of continuous creation, of what is living, as opposed to a supralunar time in which everything always leads back to the same, the self-identical. True life, that against which death can do nothing, is permanently newness and difference, not repetition and identity. In his collection *Gabriel's Wing*, he wrote this verse:

> The Prophet's "Miraj" has taught me that heaven
> Lies within the bounds of human reach.
> This universe, perhaps, is yet incomplete,
> For I hear repeated sounds of "Be, and It Was."[8]

Note here the way the poet, in these lines, presents the meaning of the *Mi'rāj*, the prophetic ascension: it is not the truth that descends from the heavens, but on the contrary the sublunar time of life that overflows into the heavens which lie "within the bounds of human reach," in order to teach it incompleteness and show it that the creative word, the divine *fiat*, "Be," is always in action, time after time after time. It is no longer the impassive world of the stars whose immobile time dominates the world of generation; it is the time of the biological that imposes its pulsations onto astronomy to absorb it into a cosmology of *élan vital*. As one of Iqbal's verses says, "Living dust thou art, not a slave of the stars."[9]

We should not think that this is simply the result of Bergson's influence, the expression in poetry by the Indian philosopher of a cosmology of emergence inspired by the author of *Creative Evolution*. He claims that this cosmology is in the Qur'an itself, and to this end he cites many verses, all of which give the world's meaning as incompletion and continued creation. Thus he refers to verse 29:19, which says, "Have they not observed how God originates creation and then revives it? Such is an easy matter for God." Verse 35:1 as well: "He adds to His creation what He wills." Other verses might also be evoked, all of which reveal the world made by God as permanent innovation, as the dream, always, of a new birth.

What accounts for the considerable importance of Iqbal's thought, and establishes it as a horizon for all modernist philosophy in Islam today, is precisely that it is wholly based on this reading of Quranic cosmology as a movement of continual emergence. And it is because of this that the "reconstruction" of thought in Islam should be seen as the liberation of a movement that had been petrified, not as the grafting, from the outside, of a modernity—reduced to its technical signs—onto an immobile essence.

The reactive fundamentalists are "modern" in this sense, in the spirit of cobbling things together, while Iqbal takes things at the root by insisting one must first of all proceed to a true philosophical self-reappraisal as movement. Conservative forces, very powerful in Muslim societies, have established a fear of innovation. The very word *innovation* has become, in fact, synonymous with "blameworthy innovation," since this blame is attached simply to the fact that one differs from a model that has itself been created by *retrospective stubbornness*.

In bringing to light an emergent cosmology that forbids vilifying time, that is to say, negating its creative aspect and seeing it only as what corrodes what had been "in those times," the Indian poet's ambition was to restore thought to its place by showing that it is not the welcoming of difference but, on the contrary, the refusal of innovation, of the very movement of life, that is, *infidelity*.

To say of the world that it is incomplete is to say that it is open to the transformative action of the human. In this action, he aims at his own completion, which consists in bringing into being an *individual*. The question of individuality, central to Muhammad Iqbal's thought, makes room for, according to what he wrote in *The Development of Metaphysics in Persia*, two opposed philosophical positions that together form the following metaphysical alternative: either ontological pluralism or a monism of being in which no act of creation can cause the ultimate Being to come out from itself.

An example of this alternative, according to the Indian philosopher, is the answer Leibniz's monadology gave to the monism of Spinozan substance. His own thinking of the individual (or of the *ego*, or of the *self*) inscribes itself within the pluralist reaction to the monism of being, in which he sees the metaphysics of a Sufism, which he rejects in the name of a philosophy of action. Iqbal's world is a universe of monads, and he is also in agreement with Leibniz in saying that what is truly not *one* being is also not, truly, one *being*. Being is for him, in effect, a tension toward unity, toward the self, toward what is, in the human, personality.

Bergson had written that the tendency toward individuation is a characteristic property of life. He sees it at work everywhere in the organic world, while at the same time he notes the contrary tendency, which goes toward repetition or reproduction. The individual is not perfectly completed as such, he wrote at the beginning of *Creative Evolution*, unless there is no part of the organism that could be detached from it and be able to live separately. But the consequence of this would be to render reproduction impossible. Thus, one can say of individuality that it carries its enemy inside itself. Individuality ultimately never exists as a state; once again, it is a tension that is capable of degrees and never fully realized, not even in the human, Bergson writes.

The Iqbalian thought of becoming-individual constructs a convergence between Quranic cosmology and Bergsonism. The only complete individual, says the poet, the only perfect ego, is the One, who does not have the opposing tendency to go out from itself. It is total, incomparable, and unique. Different from the divine "I am," that of the human, still imperfect as a living unity, is incompleteness, aspiration toward increased unity and thus increased being. All of creation is thus arranged along a scale of degrees of realization of individuality, and only what can declare "I am," Iqbal says, truly exist. "I am, I exist" is not to be found in solitude and meditation as the exception to the hypothesis of an evil genius. The Iqbalian "I am" conquers itself and constructs itself in the action of transforming the world, in order to lead it to its completion.

The Indian philosopher's poetry abounds in images expressing this movement toward the unity of self in which being *consists*. Thus, he writes that the wave exists only while it is sculpted by its own movement, and "when the mountain loses its self / it becomes a mound of sand." The human has as its vocation to be God's collaborator in the infinite work of completing the world. Because the cosmic movement attains consciousness of itself in the human, this latter receives the responsibility of accompanying it with its own action. The objective face of this action is the task of transforming the world where the human ego discovers what it means to continue creation. Iqbal presents this dialogue of man with God:

> You made the night, I made the lamp that lights it up
> You fashioned clay; I made of it a drinking cup.
> You made the wilderness, the mountain and the steppe;
> I fashioned garden, orchard, avenue and scape.
> I change dread poisons into panaceas, and
> I am the one who fashions mirrors out of sand.[10]

In the "I am the one" is found the subjective face of action, the way in which it reveals to the human the personality that he carries, or rather that he has the mission and responsibility to conquer. Like Afghani, but in what we could call a more philosophical manner, Iqbal rages against retrospective stubbornness and the contemplative attitude. Both constitute a betrayal of what one ought to be, an ignorance of what is implied by the deposit confided to humanity. Thus, with many Quranic citations, the poet recalls what it means that "the human is God's chosen" (cf. 20:122, which says of Adam that "his Lord elected him"): that, despite all his faults, the human has as his mission to be the lieutenant – in the etymological sense—of God on earth (2:28 and 6:165), because it has received the deposit that he alone among created beings accepted, to his risk and peril: "We offered the Trust to the heavens, the earth and the mountains, but they declined to carry it and were afraid of it, but man carried it— and he has ever been unjust, intemperate" (33:72).

For Iqbal, this "trust" or deposit is that of personality and freedom. The human is thus the being whose vocation is to take part in the life and freedom of the ultimate Ego that accorded her this latitude.

Sufism, in particular, sees in the human a bridge toward a completed human. Iqbal liked to understand this in comparison with what Nietzsche said of man as a continuous self-overcoming toward a higher existence. This German philosopher is therefore an important figure in his *Book of Eternity*, among the characters the poet encounters on his voyage across the heavens, along the model of Dante's *Divine Comedy* or of the *Mi'rāj*. Nietzsche there is compared to a central figure in the history of Sufism, al-Ḥallāj, who was executed in Baghdad in 922, accused of heresy for having declared "I am the truth." This martyr of Sufism became, in Iqbal's thought, a witness to the philosophy of the free individual, on the condition that he first of all be disengaged from the pantheistic interpretation that had been given to his "passion." His identification with the "truth" is not the drunkenness of a drop of water seeing itself becoming the ocean through absorption. It is not the madness of the moth that dies to itself by throwing itself into the flame, in an image common in Sufi poetry. On the contrary, said Iqbal, who praised Louis Massignon's work of reconstructing the meaning of this "passion," it is the affirmation of the consistence and permanence of the human ego once it becomes realized as personality.

The Sufism of the *vita contemplativa*, which believes that the goal is to *see* in order to then lose oneself in what is contemplated, is the opposite of what the deposit confided to the human demands. What is needed is not to *see* but to *be*, confronting the harsh reality of an open world to be transformed. This is how the meaning of the prophetic ascension should be understood, Iqbal suggests:

What is Ascension? The desire for a witness,
an examination face-to-face of a witness
a competent witness without whose confirmation
life to us is like color and scent to a rose.
In that Presence no man remains firm,
or if he remains, he is of perfect assay.
Give not away one particle of the glow you have,
knot tightly together the glow within you;
fairer it is to increase one's glow,
fairer it is to test oneself before the sun;
then chisel anew the crumbled form;

make proof of yourself; be a true being!
Only such an existent is praiseworthy,
otherwise the fire of life is mere smoke.[11]

Iqbal cites these verses at the end of *The Reconstruction of Religious Thought in Islam*. They are taken from his *Book of Eternity*, where they form part of an explanation by the Persian mystic poet Rūmī of the "mystery of the Mirāj." Iqbal saw himself, beyond all the other influences to which he had opened himself, as the disciple of this poet of the thirteenth century, who is the guide for the voyage across the heavens that makes up the *Javid-Nama*, the *Book of Eternity*. Two lessons come to us from Rūmī, who teaches how to philosophize in Islam today in order to create a future and open societies. The first lesson is that we must incorporate evolution as a way of thinking, an evolutionary thinking that makes us capable (as Father Teilhard de Chardin wrote, building on Bergson) of seeing in Duration, that is to say, in "biological Space-time."[12] The Indian poet found this thought in Rūmī; he often meditates on the following verses:

First man appeared in the class of inorganic things,
Next he passed there from into that of plants.
For years he lived as one of the plants,
Remembering naught of his inorganic state so different;
And when he passed from the vegetative to the animal state
He had no remembrance of his state as a plant,
Except the inclination he felt to the world of plants,
Especially at the time of spring and sweet flowers.
Like the inclination of infants towards their mothers,
Which know not the cause of their inclination to the breast . . .
Again the great Creator, as you know,
Drew man out of the animal into the human state.
Thus man passed from one order of nature to another,
Till he became wise and knowing and strong as he is now.
Of his first souls he has now no remembrance.
And he will be again changed from his present soul.[13]

The second lesson is that evolution is also a continuous strengthening of individuality. In these two lessons of Rūmī's is concentrated, in effect, the whole meaning of the philosophy of movement and incompletion through which Iqbal sets out to reconstruct the religious thought of Islam: ascension is the very thrust of life toward the consistency and unity of an "I am" born from action; the world is open and it continues to move toward its youth; and this is why society must always move toward more openness and the emancipation of all: to understand the movement, so as to move toward reform.

10

PLURALISM

The open is the undetermined or the unlimited. It is also the plural. Thinking in favor of movement and openness—which this book has understood as the meaning of "philosophizing in Islam"—is thus equally thinking in favor of pluralism. Let us return, to this end, to the tradition of the seventy-three sects that, we recall, Ghazālī made use of in his *Deliverance from Error* to show the urgency of choosing the one exclusively promised to salvation. We can recall, as well, the zeal the theologian put into the defense and illustration, in the troubled era in which he lived, of the "good" Sunni sect, supported by the "true" Ash'arite theology. But was he no more than a sectarian champion of official orthodoxy? Or was he this essentially? Let us put the question differently: at the end of his doubt, both existential and methodological, had he been able to establish on sure foundations which was the good sect, to the exclusion of all others? And was this the only thing that he *truly* sought to do?

If the answer to which he arrived at the end of his route indicates what the question was that *truly* troubled him, then what he was in search of was not the one orthodox sect, but the peace of a heart that had set out by detaching itself from all sectarian belonging. If his *Deliverance from Error* is read as it invites us to, that is as the *Confessions* (this Augustinian title has been used for an English translation of the work) of someone who says "I" and not "we," then perhaps one will note that what is sought out and what is found is something that goes well beyond the seventy-three sects. Or should it rather be said that it was present in each of them?

The truth of the tradition of the seventy-three sects, on reflection, is not exclusion but pluralism, or put otherwise the capacity to reach a nonsectarian understanding of truth and being attentive to the ways in which it is presented in each of the sects and outside of them. Thus one could say that from out of the seventy-three factions of which the tradition speaks, the one that will be saved is the seventy-fourth, the faction situated outside all the others; this sect beyond sects, which exists only virtually, is made up of all those who, though members of the seventy-three, know how to step outside of themselves and of a representation of belonging that is at once imprisoning and exclusive.

In *The Decisive Criterion for Distinguishing Islam from Masked Infidelity*, Ghazālī unequivocally condemns fanaticism and the excess of sects who exchange mutual accusations of infidelity,[1] and declares those who pretend that doctrinal difference is a sign of unbelief to be ignorant and stupid. If he continues to keep the philosophers at a distance in the name of the principle that one should not "[confuse] the minds of the masses,"[2] he is totally opposed to the exclusivist and intolerant interpretation of the tradition of the seventy-three sects that he had seemed to give earlier. He even offers here a radically different version. In fact, concerning the prophetic saying about the inevitable effects of time and the force of circumstances that lead to the multiplication of divergences, according to the version Ghazālī cites here, here is what it says in reality: "My community will divide into over seventy sects; all of them will enter Paradise except the Crypto-infidels."[3]

A prophetic tradition on plurality and difference, of which some have given a negative, sectarian, and exclusive version, while others have transmitted a positive, pluralist, and inclusive version—who was it, then, who misheard? Who has the correct version? There are many cases where the actions, gestures, or words of the apostle of Islam have been conveyed with variants, but here we seem to be in the presence of a pure and simple contradiction, that is, unless in the first case it is understood that the sect that will be saved is the one that is able to welcome difference, and whose members may be found in each of the groups, and in the second, it is understood that the only ones who deny themselves salvation are those who have, precisely, a radical dualist, Manichean vision of difference:[4] whoever is not with me is rejected into the outer darkness.

This substitution, for the question of the historical truth of one version against the other, of an interpretation that reconciles their meanings may also be authorized by other attested traditions that go so far as to celebrate divergence as a mercy. It is to this celebration that Ghazālī's path ultimately invites us; and, rather than the figure of the champion of an orthodoxy that is nowhere to be found, this is what truly makes him a "proof of Islam."

So then, a pluralist philosophy to reconcile the sects that have historically fractured the world of Islam and continue to do so today? What about (re)conciliation with other religions? Or even with the "infidels"?

Let us now transport ourselves to the beginning of the 1930s, in a Mali that was under French colonial domination, and more precisely to the small city of Bandiagara, founded in 1770 by a Dogon hunter and developed into the capital of the Islamized Toucouleur empire by the successors of Al Hajj Umar Tall (1797–1864), its founder. In this city lived and taught a master of Islamic sciences. The grandnephew of Al Hajj Umar Tall, he was named Bokar, son of Salif Tall, and was called "Tierno," "master" in the Fulani language. He was a dignitary of the Sufi path called the *tijaniyya*, named after its founder, Cheikh Aḥmed al-Tijānī (born in Aïn Mahdi, in Algeria, in 1737, and buried in Fez, in Morocco, in 1815). To his disciples he taught the text of the Qur'an, its commentary, and the elements of law, theology, and Sufism. Above all he offered them an example of the pious and simple life of a man constantly occupied with reading the signs and lessons inscribed in human and animal behaviors. His most celebrated disciple, Amadou Hampâté Bâ (1901–91), who was also his biographer, named him with reason "the sage of Bandiagara."[5] No doubt, Tierno was not a philosopher, if one understands by this someone trained to dialogue with established philosophies. But he knew how to listen to the eternally creative word, the one expressed in the human as well as in a dog or a bird, which continually causes it to be. And this, too, is philosophizing in Islam.

It was to this sage that one of his disciples posed the question of pluralism in religion. It was not only a question of tolerance, but a matter of knowing if plurality carries a lesson: " 'Tierno,' I asked him one day, 'is it good to converse with people of another faith to exchange ideas and better understand their god?' "[6] To this question the master responded with the lesson of tolerance that Sufism carries in its essence, since its metaphysics is founded on the conviction that, "in its Essence, Faith is one, whatever the religion that conveys it might be."[7] No doubt, one can imagine that the faith in God that often divides humans and casts them one against the other also creates a sort of fraternity between the faithful, beyond the different forms their faiths take. But can a pluralism founded on this conviction, that it is the same truth that is manifested under different faces of belief, be expanded even to embrace irreligion?

Or again, does God love the infidel? This is, in fact, the way that the question of a fully developed pluralism is posed by the disciple of the sage of Bandiagara: "Tierno, you always speak of God's love which embraces everything. But does God love infidels?"[8] "Yes" was still the master's response, contrary, he said, to the distinctions that obsess the people he called "those attached to the letter,"[9] who thus betray the One in whose name they claim to speak and who, for His part, is generosity toward the children of Adam without "distinguishing their states." And his "yes" is indeed what philosophy teaches: the wisdom of love.

CONCLUSION

I n an issue dated January 28, 2017, the French newspaper *Le Monde* reported on a rally by philosophy teachers in Morocco against newly revised textbooks in Islamic education. They had been shocked, the article said, to find in a textbook for junior high school students, under the chapter heading "Philosophy and Faith," a definition of philosophy as "a product of human thought contrary to Islam." In fact, that is a quotation from a thirteenth-century figure, an Iraqi religious leader in the study of tradition, Ibn as-Salah ash-Shahrazuri (d. 1245), mainly known for his violent attacks against philosophy. For that reason his name is often associated with that of Ghazālī but, as we have seen, it is unfair to the latter to consider his positions—in the plural, as they varied from one work to another—to be the same as the fulminations against *falsafa* of ash-Shahrazuri, who went as far as opposing logic, the science of valid reasoning, because he saw in it the Trojan horse of philosophical examination.[1]

The members of the Moroccan Association of Philosophy Teachers organized sit-ins to denounce an attack against freedom of thought, which they also saw as an attack against democracy, and declared that they were appalled to see a resurgence of misology in a modern Muslim country like Morocco, often associated with the idea of an open, dynamic Islam. In response, the ministry of education made it clear that the textbook was just quoting ash-Shahrazuri as an illustration of one given position on the question of the relationship between philosophy and faith, to be submitted to the students' examination and critical thinking.

At any rate, that crisis about textbooks conveys two main lessons concerning the teaching of philosophy (in particular the history of philosophy) in Muslim countries and everywhere.

The Moroccan teachers, swift to oppose anything that looked like an attack on their discipline in the name of freedom of thought and democracy, are right to refute the notion that Islam as such is in opposition to philosophical thinking. In so doing they are speaking on behalf of the long intellectual and spiritual history of examining and questioning that also defines Islam and that was constituted during centuries in openness to and conversations with other intellectual traditions and figures: Plato, Aristotle, or Plotinus yesterday, Nietzsche, Bergson, and others today. That such a tradition should be found in textbooks as a heritage to be transmitted to students in Muslim countries is the first lesson to be learned from the Moroccan teachers' protests.

A second lesson to be drawn from them concerns the study of philosophy everywhere. What the intellectual tradition of *falsafa* manifests is that the history of philosophy as it was constructed mainly in nineteenth-century Europe as quintessentially "Western"—Greek, then Roman, then Christian European, then modern-European—is a misleading simplification. Medieval thought coined the phrase *translatio studiorum* to express the idea that Greek sciences had been transferred to Rome and from Rome to the Christian Western European world. What Islamic philosophy among other intellectual traditions teaches us is that *translatio studiorum* is also a trajectory from Athens to Baghdad, to Cordoba, to Fez, to Timbuktu in present-day Mali. Generally speaking, there is no such thing as a unique European philosophical telos, and textbooks on the history of philosophy should reflect the fact that philosophical thought is found in every human culture. So on important notions such as "truth," "reason," "belief," "life," and so on, they should restore, for the critical thinking of students, the conversations that philosophers from different traditions have entertained.

To this double aspect of the question of textbooks on the history of philosophy and the stakes of it, it was the purpose of this book to contribute.

NOTES

INTRODUCTION

1. In addition to this new introduction, a new conclusion has been written for this English translation.
2. A few classics in the field can be quoted here as examples: Seyyed Hossein Nasr and Oliver Leaman, eds., *History of Islamic Philosophy* (London: Routledge, 2001); Seyyed Hussein Nasr, *Islamic Philosophy from Its Origin to the Present: Philosophy in the Land of Prophecy* (Albany: State University of New York Press, 2006); Majid Fakhry, *A History of Islamic Philosophy* (New York: Columbia University Press, 2004); Henry Corbin, *History of Islamic Philosophy* (London: Routledge, 2014).
3. See Alexis Kagamé, *La philosophie bantu-rwandaise de l'être*, Tome XII, I (Brussels: Collection des Mémoires de l'Académie Royale des Sciences d'Outre-Mer, 1956); and Émile Benveniste, "Categories of Thought and Language," in *Problems in General Linguistics*, trans. Mary Elizabeth Meek (Coral Gables: University of Miami Press, 1971).

1. AND HOW TO NOT PHILOSOPHIZE?

1. The Qur'an often calls to "people of understanding" to reflect on the signs of God. See for example Qur'an 3:190.

2. The Quran (18:60–82) narrates the story of the encounter between Moses and a mysterious character, known as Khidr in the Islamic Tradition, who shows him, through his apparently senseless behavior in a series of events, why the ways of God are incomprehensible to the finite understanding of the human being. Khidr, for example, kills a young man they encounter apparently for no reason before he explains at the end of their journey together that the youth, had he lived, would have caused the ruin of his parents, who were good people of faith. Different acts on the same pattern are accomplished by Khidr, who has a perception of the secret of time before it unfolds and the paradoxes of Life from a special knowledge given to him by God.

3. The Qur'an (2:30) narrates that the angels questioned God's decision to create a "vicegerent on earth" in fear that the human, thus endowed with God's attribute of freedom, would bring mischief and violence while they have one role and only one: praise and glorify the Lord.

4. Quotations from the Qur'an are taken from Tarif Khalidi's translation: Tarif Khalidi, trans., *Qur'an* (New York: Penguin, 2008).

5. Malek Chebel, *L'Islam et la raison: Le combat des idées* (Paris: Perrin, 2006), 38.

6. Seyyed Hossein Nasr, *Islamic Philosophy from Its Origin to the Present: Philosophy in the Land of Prophecy* (New York: State University of New York Press, 2006), 124.

2. HOW A LANGUAGE BECOMES PHILOSOPHICAL

1. This version of al-Ma'mun's dream, from Nādim's *Catalogue* composed at the end of the tenth century, is cited here from Jean Jolivet's "Esquisse d'un Aristote arabe" [Sketch of an Arab Aristotle], in *Penser avec Aristote* (Toulouse: Erès, 1991), 177.

2. See Jolivet, *L'Islam, la philosophie et les sciences* (Paris: Unesco, 1981).

3. Alain de Libera, *La philosophie médiévale* (Paris: Presses universitaires de France, 1993), 54.

4. Libera, 54.

5. See Cicero, *On Moral Ends*, trans. Raphael Wood (Cambridge: Cambridge University Press, 2001).

6. See Marc Bergé, *Pour un humanisme vécu: Abū Hayyān al-Tawhīdī* (Damascus: Institut français de Damas, 1979).

7. Abdurrahman Badawi, *La transmission de la philosophie grecque au monde arabe* (Paris: Vrin, 1987), 21.

8. Abdelali Elamrani-Jamal, *Logique aristotélicienne et grammaire arabe* (Paris: Vrin, 1983), 151.

9. Émile Benveniste, *Problems in General Linguistics*, trans. Mary Elizabeth Meek (Coral Gables, FL: University of Miami Press, 1971), 55–64.

10. Abdelali Elamrani-Jamal, *Logique aristotélicienne et grammaire arabe*, 151.

11. Benveniste, *Problems in General Linguistics*, 55.

12. Benveniste, 63.

13. Diagne provides the French equivalents *Qu'est-ce que l'être* and *être* to translate his English examples.—TRANS.

14. Benveniste, *Problems in General Linguistics*, 62.

15. Abderrahman al-Akhdari, *Le Soullam: Traité de logique* (Algiers, 1921).

3. WHAT DOES IT MEAN FOR A PHILOSOPHY TO BE ISLAMIC?

1. Peter Heath, *Allegory and Philosophy in Avicenna (Ibn Sīnā), with a Translation of the Book of the Prophet Muhammad's Ascent to Heaven* (Philadelphia: University of Pennsylvania Press, 1922).

2. Salomon Munk, *Mélanges de philosophie juive et arabe* (Paris: Vrin, 1998), 351.

3. Heath, *Allegory and Philosophy in Avicenna*, 111.

4. I have generally translated the French *esprit*, which can mean "spirit" or "mind," as spirit, except where the context makes "mind" a clearly better choice. Readers should bear this range of meaning in mind, though, and avoid too much of a "spiritualizing" reading.—TRANS.

5. Avicenne, *La Métaphysique du Shifa* (Paris: Vrin, 1985), 2:177.

6. Avicenne, 2:177.

7. Avicenne, 2:177.

4. AGAINST PHILOSOPHY?

1. Al-Ghazālī, *Deliverance from Error and Mystical Union with the Almightly*, trans. Muhammad Abūlaylah (Washington, DC: Center for Research in Values and Philosophy, 2001).

2. Al-Ghazālī, 61–62.

3. Al-Ghazālī, 73.

4. Al-Ghazālī, *Letter to a Disciple*, trans. Tobias Mayer (Cambridge: Islamic Texts Society, 2005), 24.

5. *Ibn Sina's* Remarks and Admonitions: Physics and Metaphysics, *an Analysis and Annotated Translation*, trans. Shams C. Inati (New York: Columbia University Press, 2014), 102.

6. Ameer Ali, *The Spirit of Islam: A History of the Evolution and Ideals of Islam, with a Life of the Prophet* (London: Chatto and Windus, 1974).

7. Ali, 469.

5. A LESSON IN ECOLOGICAL PHILOSOPHY

1. *Ibn Tufayl's Hayy Ibn Yaqzān*, ed. and trans. Lenn Evan Goodman (Los Angeles: Gee Tee Bee, 1996), 97.

2. *Avicenna on Theology*, trans. A. J. Arberry (London: John Murray, 1951).

3. *Hayy Ibn Yaqzān*, 158.

4. Diagne's phrase here, " ils les traduisent et les trahissent," echoes the famous maxim *traduttore traditore*, "to translate is to betray," and shares something of its homophony.—TRANS.

6. THE OBLIGATION TO PHILOSOPHIZE

1. Barry S. Kogan, *Averroes and the Metaphysics of Causation* (Albany: State University of New York Press, 1985), 11. This is Kogan's translation from the historian al-Marrākushī.

2. Averroes, *The Decisive Treatise and Epistle Dedicatory*, trans. Charles E. Butterworth (Provo, UT: Brigham Young University Islamic Translation Series, 2002).

3. Suhrawārdī, *The Philosophy of Illumination*, trans. John Wallbridge and Hossein Ziai (Provo, UT: Brigham Young University Islamic Translation Series, 2000).

   The word *ishrāq* in the title permits interpretation either as "Eastern" or as "illumination," since the Arabic root *sh-r-q* refers both to the East and to the sun's rising. Diagne, like Suhrawārdī or Avicenna, is playing here with this polysemy.—TRANS.

4. See his introduction to Suhrawārdī, *Le livre de la sagesse orientale* (Lagrasse: Verdier, 1986), 9.

7. THE NEED FOR PHILOSOPHY

1. Ernest Renan, "Islamism and Science," in *Orientalism: Early Sources*, vol. 1, *Readings in Orientalism*, ed. Bryan S. Turner (New York: Routledge, 2000), 200.

2. Renan, "Islamism and Science," 201.

3. Renan, "Islamism and Science," 206.
4. Renan, "Islamism and Science," 217.
5. Nikki Keddie, *Sayyid Jamāl ad-Dīn "al-Afghānī": A Political Biography* (Berkeley: University of California Press, 1972).
6. Renan, "Islamism and Science," 213.
7. Nikki Keddie, *An Islamic Response to Imperialism: Political and Religious Writings of Sayyid Jamāl ad-Dīn "al-Afghānī"* (Berkeley: University of California Press, 1968), 187.
8. Keddie, *An Islamic Response to Imperialism*, 103.
9. Alexandre Koyré describes the rise of modern science and the end of the Aristotelian cosmology as the passage from "the closed world" to "the infinite universe." Alexandre Koyré, *From the Closed World to the Infinite Universe* (New York: Harper, 1957).
10. Koyré, *From the Closed World to the Infinite Universe*, 106.

8. THE PHILOSOPHY OF REFORM

1. Muhammad Abduh, *The Theology of Unity*, trans. Ishaq Musa'ad and Kenneth Cragg (London: Allen and Unwin, 1966).
2. Syed Ameer Ali, *The Spirit of Islam: A History of Evolution and Ideals of Islam* (Delhi: B. I., 1978), 227ff. For a recent study on Ameer Ali, see Ramatoulaye Diagne, *Le modernisme en islam: Introduction à la pensée de Sayyid Amir Ali* (Paris: L'Harmattan, 2016).
3. Ali, *The Spirit of Islam*, 229–30.
4. Ali Abdel Razek, *Islam and the Foundations of Political Power*, trans. Maryam Loutfi and Abdou Filali-Ansari (Edinburgh: Edinburgh University Press, 2012), 51.
5. Razek, *Islam and the Foundations of Political Power*, 46.

9. THE PHILOSOPHY OF MOVEMENT

1. The reference is to Paul Valéry's poem "Le cimétière marin," usually translated as "The Cemetery by the Sea."—TRANS.
2. Published in English as *Time and Free Will: An Essay on the Immediate Data of Consciousness*, trans. F. L. Pogson (London: Allen and Unwin, 1921).
3. Henri Bergson, *Creative Evolution*, trans. Arthur Mitchell (New York: Holt, 1911), 2.
4. Muhammad Iqbal, *Letters and Writings of Iqbal* (Karachi: Iqbal Academy, 1967), 103.

5. Muhammad Iqbal, *The Development of Metaphysics in Persia: A Contribution to the History of Muslim Philosophy* (London: Luzac, 1908).

6. Charles Taylor, preface to *Islam and Open Society: Fidelity and Movement in the Philosophy of Muhammad Iqbal*, by Souleymane Bachir Diagne, trans. Melissa McMahon (Dakar: CODESRIA, 2010).

7. Muhammad Iqbal, *The Reconstruction of Religious Thought in Islam* (Oxford: Oxford University Press, 1934), 10.

8. Muhammad Iqbal, *Gabriel's Wing*, trans. Naeem Siddiqi, www.allamaiqbal.com/works/poetry/urdu/bal/translation/part02/03.htm.

9. Iqbal, www.allamaiqbal.com/works/poetry/urdu/bal/translation/part02/21.htm.

10. Muhammad Iqbal, *The Message of the East*, trans. M. Hadi Hussein, www.allamaiqbal.com/works/poetry/persian/payam/translation/part02/23.htm.

11. Muhammad Iqbal, *Javid-Nama*, trans. A. J. Arberry (London: Allen and Unwin, 1966), 15.

12. Pierre Teilhard de Chardin, *The Human Phenomenon*, trans. Sarah Appleton-Weber (Sussex: Brighton Academic Press, 1999), 152.

13. Cited in Iqbal, *The Reconstruction of Religious Thought in Islam*, 115.

10. PLURALISM

1. Sherman A. Jackson, *On the Boundaries of Theological Tolerance in Islam: Abū Ḥāmid al-Ghāzalī's Fayṣal al-Tafriqa Bayna al-Islām wa al-Zandaqa* (Oxford: Oxford University Press, 2002), 88–89.

2. Jackson, *On the Boundaries of Theological Tolerance in Islam*, 109.

3. Jackson, *On the Boundaries of Theological Tolerance in Islam*, 111.

4. The French translation of Ghazālī that Diagne uses translates *al-zandaqa* and *zindīq*, which Jackson renders as "masked infidelity" and "crypto-infidels," in terms of "Manichaean" or "dualism." These terms, borrowed early on from Persian, initially referred to these groups but came to have a general sense of heresy. For a brief summary, see the entry on *zindīq* in *The New Encyclopedia of Islam*, ed. Cyril Hassé (New York: Rowman and Littlefield, 2008), 491–92.—TRANS.

5. Amadou Hampâté Bâ, *A Spirit of Tolerance: The Inspiring Life of Tierno Bokar*, trans. Fatima Jane Casewit (Bloomington, IN: World Wisdom, 2008).

6. Bâ, *A Spirit of Tolerance*, 128.

7. Bâ, *A Spirit of Tolerance*, 134.

8. Bâ, *A Spirit of Tolerance*, 122.

9. Bâ, *A Spirit of Tolerance*, 127.

CONCLUSION

1. Ash-Shahrazuri is often quoted by scholars who, following the essay by Ignaz Goldziher, translated from the original German as "The Attitude of Orthodox Islam Toward the 'Ancient Sciences'" (in *Studies on Islam*, ed. and trans. Merlin L. Swartz [Oxford: Oxford University Press, 1981]), want to emphasize a natural opposition of "orthodoxy" in Islam to philosophical and scientific inquiry. Dimitri Gutas has demonstrated that this is just a preconception and simplification reinforced by the choice of dropping from the English translation of the title of Goldziher's essay the word *ancient*: Goldziher's title speaks of "The Attitude of *Ancient* Orthodox Islam." See Dimitri Gutas, *Greek Thought, Arabic Culture: The Graeco-Arabic Translation Movement in Baghdad and Early 'Abbāsid Society, 2nd–4th/8th–10th Centuries* (New York: Routledge, 1998).

BIBLIOGRAPHY

Abdel Razek, Ali. *Islam and the Foundations of Political Power.* Translated by Maryam Loutfi and Abdou Filali-Ansari. Edinburgh: Edinburgh University Press, 2012.

Abduh, Muhammad. *The Theology of Unity.* Translated by Ishaq Musa'ad and Kenneth Cragg. London: Allen and Unwin, 1966.

Al-Akhdari, Abderrahman. *Le Soullam: Traité de logique.* Translated by J. D. Luciani. Algiers: J. Carbonel, 1921.

Al-Ghazālī. *Deliverance from Error and Mystical Union with the Almightly.* Translated by Muḥammad Abūlaylah. Washington, DC: Center for Research in Values and Philosophy, 2001.

——. *Letter to a Disciple.* Translated by Tobias Mayer. Cambridge: Islamic Texts Society, 2005.

Ali, Ameer. *The Spirit of Islam: A History of the Evolution and Ideals of Islam, with a Life of the Prophet.* London: Chatto and Windus, 1974.

Averroes. *The Decisive Treatise and Epistle Dedicatory.* Translated by Charles E. Butterworth. Provo, UT: Brigham Young University Islamic Translation Series, 2002.

Avicenna. *Allegory and Philosophy in Avicenna (Ibn Sīnā), with a Translation of the Book of the Prophet Muhammad's Ascent to Heaven.* Translated, introduction, and notes by Peter Heath. Philadelphia: University of Pennsylvania Press, 1992.

——. *Avicenna on Theology.* Translated by A. J. Arberry. London: John Murray, 1951.

——. *Ibn Sina's Remarks and Admonitions: Physics and Metaphysics, an Analysis and Annotated Translation*. Translated by Shams C. Inati. New York: Columbia University Press, 2014.

——. *La Métaphysique du Shifa*. Paris: Vrin, 1985.

Bâ, Amadou Hampâté. *A Spirit of Tolerance: The Inspiring Life of Tierno Bokar*. Translated by Fatima Jane Casewit. Bloomington, IN: World Wisdom, 2008.

Badawi, Abdurrahman. *La transmission de la philosophie grecque au monde arabe*. Paris: Vrin, 1987.

Benveniste, Émile. "Categories of Thought and Language." In *Problems in General Linguistic*, translated by Mary Elizabeth Meek. Coral Gables, FL: University of Miami Press, 1971.

Bergé, Marc. *Pour un humanisme vécu: Abū Hayyān al-Tawhīdī*. Damascus: Institut français de Damas, 1979.

Bergson, Henri. *Creative Evolution*. Translated by Arthur Mitchell. New York: Holt, 1911.

——. *Time and Free Will: An Essay on the Immediate Data of Consciousness*. Translated by F. L. Pogson. London: Allen and Unwin, 1921.

Chebel, Malek. *L'Islam et la raison: Le combat des idées*. Paris: Perrin, 2006.

Cicero. *On Moral Ends*. Translated by Raphael Wood. Cambridge: Cambridge University Press, 2001.

Corbin, Henry. *History of Islamic Philosophy*. London: Routledge, 2014.

De Libera, Alain. *La philosophie medieval*. Paris: Presses universitaires de France, 1993.

Diagne, Ramatoulaye. *Le modernism en islam: Introduction à la pensée de Sayyid Amir Ali*. Paris: L'Harmattan, 2016.

Diagne, Souleymane Bachir. *Islam and Open Society: Fidelity and Movement in the Philosophy of Muhammad Iqbal*. Translated by Melissa McMahon. Dakar: CODESRIA, 2010.

Elamrani-Jamal, Abdelali. *Logique aristotélicienne et grammaire arabe*. Paris: Vrin, 1983.

Fakhry, Majid. *A History of Islamic Philosophy*. New York: Columbia University Press, 2004.

Gutas, Dimitri. *Greek Thought, Arabic Culture: The Graeco-Arabic Translation Movement in Baghdad and Early 'Abbāsid Society, 2nd-4th/8th-10th Centuries*. New York: Routledge, 1998.

Ibn Tufayl. *Ibn Tufayl's Hayy Ibn Yaqzān*. Edited and translated by Lenn Evan Goodman. Los Angeles: Gee Tee Bee, 1996.

Iqbal, Muhammad. *The Development of Metaphysics in Persia: A Contribution to the History of Muslim Philosophy*. London: Luzac, 1908.

——. *Gabriel's Wing*. Translated by Naeem Siddiqi. www.allamaiqbal.com/works/poetry/urdu/bal/translation/part02/03.htm.

——. *Javid-Nama*. Translated by A. J. Arberry. London: Allen and Unwin, 1966.

——. *Letters and Writings of Iqbal*. Karachi: Iqbal Academy, 1967.

——. *The Message of the East*. Translated by M. Hadi Hussein. www.allamaiqbal .com/works/poetry/persian/payam/translation/part02/23.htm.

——. *The Reconstruction of Religious Thought in Islam*. Oxford: Oxford University Press, 1934.

Jackson, Sherman A. *On the Boundaries of Theological Tolerance in Islam: Abū Ḥāmid al-Ghāzalī's Fayṣal al-Tafriqa Bayna al-Islām wa al-Zandaqa*. Oxford: Oxford University Press, 2002.

Jambet, Christian. "Introduction." In *Le livre de la sagesse orientale*, by Suhrawārdī. Lagrasse: Verdier, 1986.

Jolivet, Jean. "Esquisse d'un Aristote arabe." In *Penser avec Aristote*. Toulouse: Erès, 1991.

Kagamé, Alexis. *La philosophie bantu-rwandaise de l'être*. Brussels: Collection des Mémoires de l'Académie Royale des Sciences d'Outre-Mer (Tome XII, I), 1956.

Keddie, Nikki. *Sayyid Jamāl ad-Dīn "al-Afghānī": A Political Biography*. Berkeley: University of California Press, 1972.

Kogan, Barry S. *Averroes and the Metaphysics of Causation*. Albany: State University of New York Press, 1985.

Koyré, Alexandre. *From the Closed World to the Infinite Universe*. New York: Harper, 1957.

Munk, Salomon. *Mélanges de philosophie juive et arabe*. Paris: Vrin, 1998.

Nasr, Seyyed Hussein. *Islamic Philosophy from Its Origin to the Present, Philosophy in the Land of Prophecy*. New York: State University of New York Press, 2006.

Nasr, Seyyed Hossein, and Oliver Leaman, eds. *History of Islamic Philosophy*. London: Routledge, 2001.

Qur'an. Translated by Tarif Khalidi. New York: Penguin, 2008.

Renan, Ernest. "Islamism and Science." In *Orientalism: Early Sources*, vol. 1, *Readings in Orientalism*, edited by Bryan S. Turner. New York: Routledge, 2000.

Suhrawārdi. *Le livre de la sagesse orientale*. Lagrasse: Verdier, 1986.

——. *The Philosophy of Illumination*. Translated by John Wallbridge and Hossein Ziai. Provo, UT: Brigham Young University Islamic Translation Series, 2000.

Teilhard de Chardin, Pierre. *The Human Phenomenon*. Translated by Sarah Appleton-Weber. Sussex: Brighton Academic Press, 1999.

INDEX

Abbasid (dynasty), 6, 36
Abdel Razek, Ali, xii, 81–84
Abduh, Muhammad, xi, 12, 71, 73,
76–78, 82
Abū Bakr (first caliph), 3
Abū Hanifa, 9
Adam, 5, 7, 94; children of, 14, 31, 56,
101
Al Afghani, Jamāl ad-Dīn Assadabādī,
xi, 79, 94; life of, 69–70; on science,
71–72, 74–75
Ali (fourth caliph), 3, 5, 36, 61
Ali, Ameer, xii, 13, 45; on justice, 81; life
of, 79–80
Allegory, 26, 44, 53, 64
Angels, 4, 27, 29, 30
Arabic language, ix, x, 7, 15, 19, 21–22;
becoming-philosophical of, 17
Arcane, discipline of the, 28, 53, 61, 62,
72
Aristotle, x, 15, 20–24, 26, 39, 57–58,
60–61, 82, 86–87, 103; Islamic
Aristotelianism and, 36; al-Ma'mun
vision of, 14
Ascent/Ascension, 28, 31, 42–43, 95, 97;
as allegory, 26; Avicenna on, 29–33;
depiction of, 30–32; meaning of,
32–33; mysticism in, 33; in the

Qur'an, 24–26; rational explication
of, 29–30. See also Mi 'rāj
Al Ash'ari, Abu Hasan, 10–11, 41, 45
Attributes (God's), 6, 8–9. See also
Names
Averroes (Abū Walīd Muḥammad ibn
Aḥmad Ibn Rushd), xi, 22, 25, 36, 40,
44, 47, 71–72; exile of, 58–59; Ghazālī
and, 60, 63; on God, 63–64; life of,
56–57, 64–66; on philosophy, 60–62;
syllogism of, 59–60; with Ibn Tufayl,
57–58
Avicenna (Abū 'Ali al-Husayn ibn
'Abdallah Ibn Sīnā), x, 22, 25–26, 28,
39, 44, 51, 65, 71; on ascension, 29–33;
Ghazālī on, 42; in Hayy Ibn Yaqzān,
47–48; mastery of, 27; on
Muhammad, 24

Bâ, Amadou Hampâté, 101
Al Basri, Hassan, 9
Bayt al Hikma (House of Wisdom), 15
Benveniste, Émile, x; on being, 20–21
Berger, Gaston, 73
Bergson, Henri, 86–87, 90, 93, 96, 103
Berkeley, George, 86
Body, 28, 32; resurrection of, 40–41
Boole, George, 21

Caliphate, 5, 47, 81–83
Categories, x, 20
Center, of the world, 27–28, 51
Chahine, Youssef, 64, 66
Chardin, Father Teilhard de, 96
Cicero, 16–17
Closure, 22; self, 33, 84. *See also* Enclosure
Community, Islamic/Muslim, 1–4, 8, 37, 44, 62–63, 72, 81, 84, 99
Copula, 21, 22
Createdness of the world, 40, 64. *See also* Eternity of the world

Dante, Alighieri, 95
Democracy, democratic, 4, 102
Descartes, René, xi, 12, 22, 75
Desire, 27; of human beings, 29; nature of, 29–30
Destiny, 89
Diderot, Denis, 48
Duration, 86–87, 96

Ego, 43, 92–95
Elan vital, 86, 91
Enclosure, 73, 79. *See also* Closure
Essence, 6, 8
Eternity, of the world, 40, 43–44
Eve, 4
Evolution, 96–97
Ewe (language), 20–21

Faculty, faculties, 26, 29, 31, 42–44; rational, 27, 28, 30, 32–33, 41
Falsafa, 15, 22, 59, 66, 103
Al Farābī, Abu Nasr, 22, 26, 33, 39
Fatalism, 6, 89
Fate, 5; fatum, 89
Fatima, 3, 36
Fatimids, 36
Faylasūf/Falāsifa, 23, 25–26, 34–35, 39, 72
Fidelity, 9, 10, 36, 54, 73, 83; to Muhammad, 3–4; philosophy of, 3–4
Filali-Ansary, Abdou, 83
Fiqh, 8
Freedom, 49; Iqbal on, 94–95; in Qur'an, 4–5; to say no, 4–5
Free will, 4–5; of qadirites, 6
Fundamentalism, 77–78

Gabriel (archangel), 24–25, 30, 31
Galileo, Galilei, 45, 72, 74
Gaon, Saadia, 22

Al Ghazālī, Abu Hamīd (Ghazali), x, xi, 47, 53, 59–60, 63, 98–100, 102; Averroes (Ibn Rushd, Abū Walīd Muḥammad ibn Aḥmad) and, 60, 63; on Avicenna, 42; crisis of, 38; on human beings, 44; Islamic Aristotelianism denunciation of, 36; life of, 36–38; on light, 42–44; on Mu'tazilism, 41–42; questioning of, 39–41; quietism of, 35, 45; on senses, 41–43; with Sunnism, 38–39, 45

Hadith, 2, 8
Al Hallaj, Husayn Mansur, 95
House of Wisdom, 15; Pluralism in, 16; purpose of, 16. *See also* Bayt al Hikma
Human, being/becoming, ix, xi, 48; complete, perfect, 32–33; desire of, 29; distinction of, 28–29; ego of, 94–95; Ghazālī on, 44; as microcosm, 44; revelation of, 33–34

Iblīs, 5
Ibn Ḥanbal, Aḥmad, 10
Ibn Khaldun, 8
Ibn Rushd. *See* Averroes
Ibn Sīnā. *See* Avicenna
Ibn Tufayl, Abu Bakr, xi, 22, 48, 52; Averroes with, 57–58; life of, 46–47; work of, 47–54
Images, 32, 62
Imagination, 25, 30–32, 42, 53, 60
Imams, imamate, 3, 45
Individual, 92–93, 95
Individuality, 92–93, 97
Individuation, 93
Infidelity, 35, 92, 99
Infidels, xii, 99–101
Innovation, 3, 8, 40, 78, 91–92
Inquisition, 10. *See also* Mihna
Intellect, 27, 29, 30, 90; prophetic, 29
Intelligence, 27–28, 31, 33; active, 27, 29, 47; prophetic, 29; universal, 29–30, 32
Intelligible world, 31, 33; prophetic, 29; realities, 25, 27, 29, 62; truth, 25, 27, 29, 62; world, 25, 27, 29, 62
Interpretation, xi, 6, 28, 32, 55–56, 58–59, 62–64, 78–79
Iqbal, Muhammad, xii, 12, 87–97; on being, 92–94; on freedom, 94–95; life

of, 87–88; Rūmī inspiration of, 96–97;
 on time, 89–91
Isrā (Night Journey), 24

Jacobite, Christians, 16
Al-Jāhiz, 18
Jambet, Christian, 66
Jerusalem, 28, 30
Jesus, 25
Jolivet, Jean, 15
Al-Jubba'I, Abū Ali Muhammad, 11
Jurisprudence, 8, 22, 37, 61. *See also Fiqh*
Al Juwaynī, Imam al Haramayn, 36, 37

Kagamé, Alexis, x
Kalam, 8–12
Kant, Immanuel, 72
Kayfa, kayfiyyah, 16. *See also* Quiddity
Keddie, Nikki, 69
Kepler, Johannes, 74
Khalif, 3–4
Khan, Muhammad Azam, 70–71
Khan, Shir Ali, 71
Khidr, 4

Language, human, 19, 22, 31, 56; of
 being, 20–21; of Ewe, 20–21; God and,
 6–7; in *Hayy Ibn Yaqzān*, 52–54; Mattā
 on, 17; of Muslim philosophy, 16–17;
 in Qur'an, 7; Al-Sīrāfī on, 17–18; truth
 in, 53–54. *See also* Arabic language;
 Translation
Law: religious, 58–59; tribal, 8
Leibniz, Wilhem Gottfried, 19, 21,
 88–89, 92–93
Libera, Alain de, 16
Literalism, 10, 51, 53
Literalists, 28, 32, 52
Literality, 62
Logic, x, 18–19, 26, 36, 39, 60; as
 instrument, 61; Sīrāfī on, 21–22

Maimonides, 7, 22
Mālik Shah, 37
Al-Ma'mun, 10, 18, 23, 33, 61, 68, 75, 87;
 Aristotle vision from, 14; on reason,
 14–15
Massignon, Louis, 95
Mattā, Abū Bishr, x, 21–22; argument
 of, 19–20; on language, 17; modernity
 of, 20; on Al-Sīrāfī, 19–20
Mecca, 24, 25, 70

Mihna *(inquisition)*, 10
Mi'rāj, 25, 33, 42, 95, 96
Modernity, x, xi, xii, 74, 76–77, 84, 85,
 92; Al-Jāhiz on, 18–19; of Mattā, 20; in
 Mu'tazilism, 13; tradition and, 78–79
Moses, 4, 25, 48
Mosque: furthest, Al Aqsā, 24, 28;
 sacred, 24, 27
Movement: of life, 2, 84, 92; philosophy
 of, 85, 97; principle of, 45, 87; spirit
 of, x, 2, 79
Muhammad (Prophet), 1–3, 8, 24–25, 79;
 companions of, 2; death of, 1–2;
 fidelity to, 3–4; with God, 24; Sīna on,
 24; successor of, 3–4
Al-Mulk, Fakhr, 38
Al-Mulk, Nizām, 37
Munk, Salomon, 26
Mu'tazilism, 18, 35; Ghazālī on, 41 42;
 modernity in, 13; oppression and, 10;
 rationalism of, 10, 41–42
Mu'tazilite, 9–11, 14, 18
Mysticism, ix, 33, 36, 38, 41, 50; in
 ascension, 33. *See also* Sufism

Names: of God, xii, 12. *See also* Attributes
Nature, ix, 51; prophetic, 33
Nestorian Christians, 16, 68
Newton, Isaac, 45, 74
Nietzsche, Friedrich, 95, 103
Night Journey, 24

Openness, xi, xii, 22, 34, 74, 97–98;
 death and, 2; of spirit, 18

Peripateticism, Islamic, 27
Person, becoming, 48, 88
Personality, 93–95
Philosophy: of Arabic language, 17;
 Averroes on, 60–62; becoming
 Islamic, 32; of fidelity, 3–4; history
 of, x; Islamic, ix, 23–24, 47, 69;
 Islamization of, 23; Mu'tazilite
 rational branch of, 10; of reform, 76;
 religion with, ix; as religious study,
 60; restoration of, 103–4. *See also*
 Falāsifa; Muslim philosophy
Plato, 15, 24, 28, 57, 82, 103
Plotinus, 103
Pluralism, xi, xii, 45, 46, 66, 86, 92,
 98–99, 101; in House of Wisdom, 16;
 philosophy of, 100

Predestination, 4, 6
Predetermination, 8
Predicate, 21
Proclus, 16
Psychology, 25–26
Ptolemy, 15

Qadr, 6
Quiddity, 17
Quietism, 35, 45; quietist, 56
Qur'an, the: ascension in, 24–26;
  freedom in, 4–5; on knowledge,
  55–56; language in, 7; Moses in,
  106n2; punctuation of, 55–56;
  questions from, 1–2; uncreatedness
  of, 10–11; understanding of, 4;
  women in, 81

Rationalism, ix, 9, 12, 45, 56;
  development of, xi; of Mu'tazilism,
  10, 41–42
Reason, 8, 23, 25, 33, 35, 40–44, 46, 48,
  61–63, 68, 71, 76, 78, 83, 104; in
  Ash'arism, 12; conformity to, 9–10;
  fear of, 9; in Hayy Ibn Yaqzān, 49–50;
  al-Ma'mun on, 14–15
Reasoning, grammar of, x
Reconstruction, x, 24, 77, 86–87, 92
Reform, xii, 13, 73, 76, 84, 97
Reformism, 45
Reformist, reformer, xi, 12, 45, 70, 73,
  75, 82
Renan, Ernest, 58, 72, 76; on science,
  67–69, 70–71, 73–74
Responsibility, human, ix, xi, 8, 95
Revelation, 2, 7, 14–15, 17, 22–23, 33–34,
  61
Rūmī, Jalāl ud-Dīn, 96–97

Sadrā, Mollā, 66, 75
Saladin, 65
Satan, 5
Sayings: prophetic, 2–3, 8. See also Hadith
Self, 30, 92–93
Sen, Amartya, 89
Senghor, Léopold Sédar, 86
Senses, 30, 40; Ghazālī on, 41–43; light
  with, 43
Sensible, 29, 32, 40; realities, 27, 31, 43, 52;
  truth, 27, 31, 43, 52; world, 27, 31, 43, 52

Ash-Shahrazuri, Ibn as-Salah, 102–3
Shi'a/shiism, 18, 36–38, 45, 66, 69, 70;
  beginning of, 3
Shirāzī, Qotboddin, 66
As-Sirāfī, Abū Said, 17–21
Socrates, 17, 21, 24
Spirit, x, 12, 28; Holy, 29–30; prophetic,
  29, 43; types of, 25, 32, 53, 58, 60, 62,
  64, 71
State, Islamic, ix
Sufism, 36, 92, 94–95, 100, 101; God
  connection in, 44–45
Suhrawārdī, 65–66
Sunna, 2–3. See also Tradition
Sunnism, 18, 37; beginning of, 3;
  dissimulation in, 69; Ghazālī with,
  38–39, 45

Tall, Al Hajj Umar, 100
Tall, Tierno Bokar Salif, xii,
  100–1
Taste, 42, 44, 47, 51
Al-Tawḥīdī, Abū Hayyān, 18
Taylor, Charles, 88
Al-Tijani, Cheikh Ahmed, 100
Time, xii, 78, 85–87, 92, 96; in
  cosmology, 93; God as, 90; Iqbal on,
  89–91
To be, 20–22. See also Copula
Tolerance, xii, 46, 65–66, 101
Tradition, 4, 33; prophetic, 37. See also
  Sunna
Translation, 19, 33, 52, 58;
  appropriation and, 18; dilemmas of,
  16; from Greek, ix; in Muslim
  philosophy, 16–17; of Sīnā, Abū 'Ali
  Ibn, x; translatio studiorum, 103

Umar (second caliph), 3
Ummayyad (dynasty), 5–6, 36
Unity, 9, 93; of God, 6; multiplicity
  with, 6
Uthmān (third caliph), 3

Valéry, Paul, 86

Word, of God, 1, 7–8, 14, 62, 91

Ya'qūb, Abū Yūsuf (al Mansūr), 58, 65
Yūsuf, Abū Ya'qūb, 47, 57

RELIGION, CULTURE, AND PUBLIC LIFE

SERIES EDITOR: KATHERINE PRATT EWING

After Pluralism: Reimagining Religious Engagement, edited by Courtney Bender and Pamela E. Klassen

Religion and International Relations Theory, edited by Jack Snyder

Religion in America: A Political History, Denis Lacorne

Democracy, Islam, and Secularism in Turkey, edited by Ahmet T. Kuru and Alfred Stepan

Refiguring the Spiritual: Beuys, Barney, Turrell, Goldsworthy, Mark C. Taylor

Tolerance, Democracy, and Sufis in Senegal, edited by Mamadou Diouf

Rewiring the Real: In Conversation with William Gaddis, Richard Powers, Mark Danielewski, and Don DeLillo, Mark C. Taylor

Democracy and Islam in Indonesia, edited by Mirjam Künkler and Alfred Stepan

Religion, the Secular, and the Politics of Sexual Difference, edited by Linell E. Cady and Tracy Fessenden

Boundaries of Toleration, edited by Alfred Stepan and Charles Taylor

Recovering Place: Reflections on Stone Hill, Mark C. Taylor

Blood: A Critique of Christianity, Gil Anidjar

Choreographies of Shared Sacred Sites: Religion, Politics, and Conflict Resolution, edited by Elazar Barkan and Karen Barkey

Beyond Individualism: The Challenge of Inclusive Communities, George Rupp

Love and Forgiveness for a More Just World, edited by Hent de Vries and Nils F. Schott

Relativism and Religion: Why Democratic Societies Do Not Need Moral Absolutes, Carlo Invernizzi Accetti

The Making of Salafism: Islamic Reform in the Twentieth Century, Henri Lauzière

Mormonism and American Politics, edited by Randall Balmer and Jana Riess

Religion, Secularism, and Constitutional Democracy, edited by Jean L. Cohen and Cécile Laborde

Race and Secularism in America, edited by Jonathon S. Kahn and Vincent W. Lloyd

Beyond the Secular West, edited by Akeel Bilgrami

Pakistan at the Crossroads: Domestic Dynamics and External Pressures, edited by Christophe Jaffrelot

Faithful to Secularism: The Religious Politics of Democracy in Ireland, Senegal, and the Philippines, David T. Buckley

Holy Wars and Holy Alliance: The Return of Religion to the Global Political Stage, Manlio Graziano

The Politics of Secularism: Religion, Diversity, and Institutional Change in France and Turkey, Murat Akan

Democratic Transition in the Muslim World: A Global Perspective, edited by Alfred Stepan